The
A B C
of
STAGE
LIGHTING

The
A B C
of
STAGE
LIGHTING

Francis Reid

A & C Black · London
Drama Book Publishers · New York

First published in 1992
A & C Black (Publishers) Limited
35 Bedford Row, London WC1R 4JH

ISBN 0-7136-3609-2

© Francis Reid 1992

Published simultaneously in the U.S.A. by
Drama Book Publishers, 260 Fifth Avenue,
New York, New York 10001.

ISBN 0-89676-119-3

CIP catalogue records for this book are available
from the British Library and the Library of
Congress.

Typeset by Florencetype Ltd, Kewstoke, Avon
Printed in Great Britain by Biddles Ltd,
Guildford, Surrey

Prologue

The language of stage lighting can often seem like an impenetrable barrier to anyone wishing to develop their understanding of the subject or to improve their communication with the specialists who practise its art and craft. Even experienced lighting people can find some of the terminology obscure.

This is perhaps inevitable with a visual art form so dependent upon complex technology: not only are visual experiences notoriously difficult to describe in words, but the pace of technological advance is such that much of the equipment becomes obsolescent before it is fully established. However, although equipment may vanish, it tends to leave a legacy in the way we work and the words we speak. Accordingly, while this glossary endeavours to assemble all the key current words and phrases, it also includes a substantial selection of references to types of equipment which, although no longer in use, still influence today's techniques through their operational philosophy.

Theatrespeak is becoming increasingly uniform in all English language countries, but an attempt has been made to incorporate significant national differences where these still exist. When alternatives are only a matter of spelling, British spelling has been adopted – theatres and colours rather than theaters and colors. America refers to the entire North American continent rather than just the United States. To avoid the text being peppered with 'qv', cross references have been restricted to occasions when the connection with another entry is not particularly obvious. Readers uncertain about the meaning of any technical term used in the text should seek an explanation under the individual alphabet entry for that term.

All entries represent the author's own understanding of what the words mean and reflect his own use of them. Although working as a lighting designer for over thirty years and trying to teach the subject for nearly as long, he has never undertaken any formal theatre studies. Consequently, it is quite probable that his personal vocabulary has acquired not just minor inaccuracies but major misconceptions! Furthermore, since theatre is a people industry, it is inevitable that some of the text may be coloured by personal experiences and opinions. In anticipation of a second edition, he invites corrections for existing entries and suggestions for additional ones.

The author is particularly indebted to Andy Collier for locating historical material in the unique archive of Strand Lighting. He also extends his grateful thanks to Strand (including Century) for many of the contemporary illustrations and to ADB, CCT, Celco, Howard Eaton, Modelbox, Pani, Rosco, Strong, Teatro, White Light.

ABTT (Association of British Theatre Technicians). A society, formed in 1961, of all those who support the actor. Through meetings, publications and specialist committees, the ABTT provides architects, designers and technicians with a means of exchanging information and opinion. The ABTT is the British arm of OISTAT. See also USITT.

A-cue An additional cue inserted, usually during technical or dress rehearsals, after sequential numbers have been allocated at the plotting session, ie Q32A will come between Q32 and Q33. Although there is no need for memory numbers to be identical with cue numbers or even be sequential, plot writing and communications are simplified if they are. Increasing sophistication of computer-based lighting controls allows extra memories to be inserted with a decimal designation, eg Q32.1, Q32.2, etc.

Accent A light which makes a positive visual statement by nature of its direction, intensity or colour.

Achromatic Lenses which do not split light into the colours of the spectrum, ie are free from CHROMATIC ABERRATION. Spotlight lenses should be achromatic although some of the more affordable lenses have a slight tendency towards a very narrow rainbow ring (often predominantly blue) around their edge.

Acting area (1) The area of the stage setting within which the actor performs. (2) An obsolete type of fixed focus instrument used for downlighting.

Adapter Short length of cable with a plug at one end and socket of a different type at the other. Used to feed equipment from a source terminating in an incompatible socket.

ADB ADB of Belgium, now owned by Siemens, are major European equipment manufacturers. The wide range of their instruments and controls for all types of stages is matched only by Strand.

Additive colour mixing See COLOUR MIXING.

Advance bar A spot bar hung within the auditorium, close to the proscenium.

Ambience   The overall atmosphere of the (stage) environment.

Ambient light   Stray uncontrolled general light, mostly generated by reflection.

Analogue   Traditional analogue control systems process and transmit information as a continuous electrical signal whereas newer digital systems process a sequence of information bits which are distinctly separate although infinitesimally short. Most modern control desks, except the very simplest, now generate digital signals but, although the newest dimmers function digitally and accept digital signals directly, most dimmers are still analogue. Consequently there is often a need for digital/analogue signal conversion. See also MULTIPLEXING and PROTOCOL.

Angles   The angle at which light hits an actor or a scenic element. This is probably the most critical factor in lighting design and, particularly for actor lighting, requires compromise between several interacting factors including illuminating, sculpting and selecting. See also BEAM ANGLE.

Angle of incidence   The angle at which a light beam hits a surface. If the surface is reflective, light will be reflected at the same angle. See also REFLECTION.

Animation discs   Large discs with break-up patterns, motor-rotated in front of profile spots fitted with gobos to produce an effect of movement.

Appia   Adolphe Appia (1862–1928). Swiss scenographer whose ideas were not only too radical to be acceptable to the theatre of his time but also, especially in lighting, ahead of the available technology. However the foundation of today's set and lighting design can be found in his illustrated writings and those of Edward Gordon Craig.

Arc   Light may be generated by electrical energy bridging the gap between a pair of conductors. Carbon rods separated by an air gap had a long run as the standard source of the brightest stage light, particularly in follow spots and scenic projectors. But carbon arcs have now been superseded by electrodes enclosed with special gases in a glass envelope. A jab of extremely high voltage is required to 'strike' the arc with an initial bridging of the gap between the electrodes. Arcs cannot be dimmed smoothly to zero by electrical means: instruments using them as a light source therefore require mechanical shuttering. In many applications, particularly follow spots, an operator is in attendance; but shutters – some are venetian blinds while others are glasses with a grey scale gradually increasing from clear to black – can be provided with motors operated from standard dimmer channels on the control desk. See also DISCHARGE LAMPS and PANI.

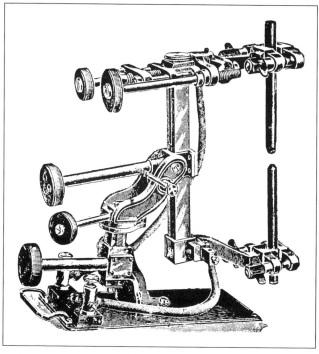

Carbon ARC mechanism with hand screw adjustments for centring the arc in the optical system and maintaining the correct gap between carbons as they burn away.

Areas Sub-divisions of the total acting area into the sections over which independent selective control of light is required. These areas are normally at actor head height which, because of the need for light to hit actors at an angle, does not correspond to floor level.

Arena stage A stage which thrusts into the auditorium so that the audience are on at least two, probably three and possibly four sides. (In America the term is restricted to a stage where the playing area is completely surrounded by audience.)

Argand The standard type of lamp used in theatres for both oil and gas lighting. Its circular wick or burner ensured a steadier brighter light by allowing a column of air to rise through a circular flame enclosed in a glass 'chimney' to protect it from draught.

Arri Major film and studio lighting manufacturers who, through a fairly recent incursion into theatre, have exercised considerable influence (in association with America's ETC/ LMI) on control board development, particularly in the area of alternative control surfaces at the interface between operator and machine.

Asbestos border Prior to recognition of the toxic hazards, aprons of asbestos cloth were often hung behind masking borders as a precaution against fire risks from heat generated by adjacent lighting equipment.

Association of Lighting Designers (ALD) A British forum for lighting designers to exchange views, both amongst themselves and with manufacturers, on all matters relating to the art and craft of their profession. The association is not a trade union: British lighting designers work under the standard contract negotiated by Equity for all designers, whether of scenery, costumes or lighting.

Atmosphere Light may be used to support and even create the atmosphere of a scene. Warm and cool tones can indicate happy and sad emotional states while the balance of light and shade can suggest many conditions from apprehension to terror. Such use of light is an important part of a package of integrated staging devices with which actor and director seek to influence the emotional response of the audience.

Auditorium lights See HOUSELIGHTS.

Autocue A 1970s memory control system where channels were accessed by pointing a light pen at the appropriate data on a video screen.

Autolight See MODELBOX.

Automated fixtures A term used by some manufacturers to describe computerised remotely focusable spotlights.

Automod A control desk facility which temporarily re- places selected channels with designated alternatives. Useful when instruments have been knocked or their lamp fila- ments have blown.

Autos 'Automatic' colour changers fitted to spotlights on balcony fronts, particularly in the 1930s, 1940s and 1950s. Four colour frames could be moved, singly or in combi- nations, by solenoids remotely activated from the control board.

Autotransformer A dimmer which controls light intensity by varying the voltage supplied to the lamp. A moving arm, rotary or sliding, makes a variable contact with a single copper wire coil wound round a soft iron core. More economical and load independent than resistance dimmers which operate by varying current to the lamp. Like all mechanical dimmers, it is now superseded by the solid state thyristor.

BC cap The simple bayonet cap of the domestic lamp is unsuitable for stage use. When domestic type general service lamps are used (mostly in battens) a screw-in base is used for safety, while all spotlights use special prefocus bases which ensure proper orientation of the filament. See also ES and PREFOCUS.

Baby spot Term used for early small spotlights, with small profiles being called BABY MIRROR SPOTS.

Backing light Illumination for 'backings' – the scenery outside doors, arches, small windows, etc.

Backlight Light coming from behind actors or pieces of scenery to sculpt and separate them from their background.

Back projection Projected background with the projector positioned either to the front or rear of the screen. See also REAR PROJECTION.

Back-up Control board facility which provides light for a performance to continue in the event of a failure, particularly amnesia, induced by the system's malfunction. Back-ups vary in sophistication from complete system duplication to the assigning of basic selections of channels to group masters.

Baffle Metal screen behind the ventilation holes in a lighting instrument to prevent light escaping.

Balance For optimum visual impact, the various components of a stage lighting picture require careful balancing. Since brightness is relative rather than absolute, we perceive the light intensity at one part of the stage by comparing it to the rest. Thus, when seeking to make one actor brighter than the rest, rather than increase the intensity on that actor, it is often more appropriate to decrease it on the others. Particularly careful balancing is required between actor and scenic environment and between colours. In making these balance judgements, lighting designers must rely on their own artist's eyes.

Balcony rail Light mounting position on the front of an auditorium balcony – particularly the highest balcony.

Ballast Discharge lamps require a current limiting ballast, normally housed in a unit adjacent to the instrument. Electronic ballasts are used to eliminate the flicker problems associated with using discharge lighting for cinematography.

Ballet Lighting for ballet places major emphasis on sculpting the dancer's body. There is therefore a larger proportion of side, top and backlighting than in drama. Lights above the stage tend to be focused across the stage rather than on the diagonals associated with drama's concentration upon actor's faces. In classical ballet there is usually little scope for selective use of lighting to determine areas because a dancer can traverse the entire stage area in a few leaps and fewer seconds.

Banks Groups of dimmers, switches or lights, mounted in close proximity. See also DIMMERBANK.

Bar (1) Horizontal metal tube of scaffolding diameter (48mm) for hanging lights (**pipe** in America). (2) Places of refreshment where light personnel foregather to discuss their profession in general and confer about the current show in particular.

Barndoors Four-shutter rotatable device added to fresnel and PC focus spots to shape the beam and reduce stray scatter light. Lower cost two-flap barndoors are occasionally used in America.

Barrel Older term, derived from gas barrel, for the flown bars from which lighting is suspended above the stage.

Base The part of a lamp through which mechanical and electrical connections are made, providing support for the filament and glass envelope.

Battens (1) Formerly known as magazine battens. Lengths of overhead compartmented floods arranged in 3 or 4 circuits for colour mixing. Called **border lights** in America. (2) Lengths of timber at the tops and bottoms of cloths. (3) Flying bars/pipes, particularly in America.

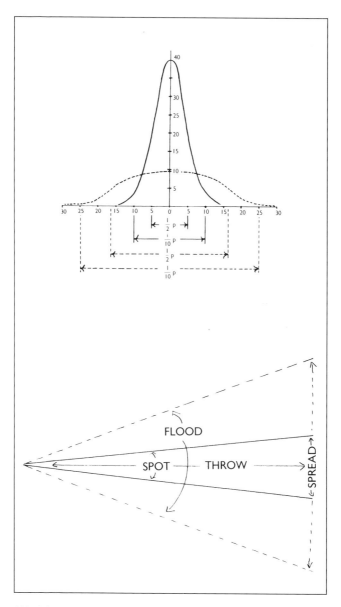

(Above)
The beam distribution of a small fresnel on its narrowest spot (solid line) and widest flood (dotted line), showing half-peak and tenth-peak BEAM ANGLES. The effective beam spread is that between the two half-peak angles, in this case from about 10° to 35°.

(Below)
These angles can be used to calculate the width of beam spread from a given throw.

Beam (1) The light emerging from a lighting instrument and passing through the air, ever diminishing in brightness, until it hits something which it illuminates. (2) In America, a lighting position in the auditorium ceiling.

Beam angle The angle of the cone of light produced by a spotlight. This 'half-peak angle' is the point in the distribution of light across the beam where intensity falls away to not less than half its maximum value – which the eye perceives as a virtually even beam. (At the 'tenth-peak' or 'field angle', intensity falls away to one tenth of its peak value; and at the 'cut-off angle', the light has fallen away to less than 1% of its maximum.) (*Illus. p. 7.*)

Beam divertors Once light has emerged from a spotlight, it travels in a straight line and cannot be made to turn corners. (Light will follow the contours of curving optical fibres, but continues in a straight line on emerging.) Only a reflective surface will divert the path of the beam. In the past, fixed spotlights with small moveable mirrors to direct their beams were sometimes mounted on lighting bridges, and this technique has been revived recently using a fixed spotlight with a motorised mirror for remote panning, tilting and focusing of the emergent beam. Beam diversion with large mirrors can be a useful way of increasing the throw of scene projectors and accommodating them to tight spaces. Small beam divertor mirrors are available for fixing to the objective lenses used with standard effects discs.

Beamlight Lensless spotlight with a parabolic reflector giving an intense parallel beam.

Beam projector American term for BEAMLIGHT.

Beam quality The major factor in the quality of light emerging from a spotlight is the degree of hardness/softness of the beam edge. In simple focus spots the edge quality is predetermined by the choice of lens (see FRESNEL, FOCUS SPOTS, PC). With profile spots the edge can be hardened or softened as required by adjustment of the lens relative to the gate. Gobos in profile spots, particularly when used in soft focus, can give a controlled degree of break-up across a light beam. The development of increasingly subtle diffuser filters is becoming a major method of fine control of beam quality – both at the edge and across the beam.

Beam shape A spotlight's conical beam produces a circular image which becomes an ellipse under normal usage with light hitting the stage floor or scenery from an oblique angle. The shape of this beam may be controlled approximately with barndoors added to the front of a simple focus or

Low Voltage BEAMLIGHT with parabolic reflector and 24 volt 500 watt silvered lamp fed from a mains voltage dimmer through an integral transformer.

fresnel spot, and precisely with the shutters incorporated in the optical system of a profile spot.

Bentham For many years Frederick Bentham (b. 1911) was synonymous with British stage lighting equipment. For some four decades he was perhaps the major English speaking (outside America) influence: all lighting control boards were either devised personally by him, or by others reacting against his teaching. Always articulate in voice and pen, retirement has induced only a partial mellowness and Fred is now active in the cause of theatre archaeology. There can be no mention of Bentham without a reference to B Bear who was the Sancho Panza to his Don Quixote during the golden years of Strand. They affected to despise modern doctrines of marketing, yet their sales approach was as successful as it was unorthodox. They enjoyed a rosy apotheosis during the final years of Twenty Nine King Street (qv) where Rank provided a saloon bar so that they could tilt at many windmills, particularly their benefactors.

Bifocal spots Profile spots with an additional set of shutters to allow a combination of hard and soft edges from the same instrument.

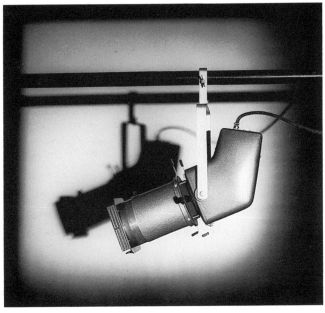

Strand Pattern 264 BIFOCAL spotlight lit by another Pattern 264 using two of the hard and two of the soft shutters.

Black light See UV.

Bleed (1) Lighting a scene behind a gauze to make the scene become gradually visible through the gauze. (2) Light visible through parts of canvas scenery which have become translucent due to paint being insufficiently opaque.

Blending Ideally, the beams for separate areas should have such smooth overlaps that they join imperceptibly. To assist this, an overall wash of light may be superimposed to 'blend' the joined areas together. However, this blending wash can often result in a muddy texture.

Blinders Lights focused into the eyes of an audience to blind them so that they will be distracted from seeing the details of a scene change.

Blind plotting Recording lighting states on a memory control system without actually activating the lights on the stage. Used to prepare a plot when the lights have not been focused or the stage set with scenery; or to prepare or modify cues without interrupting rehearsal or performance.

Blown Loss of light due to rupture of lamp filament or fuse.

Blues Working lights around the sides of the stage which remain alight during performances. They usually have blue filters to provide maximum light level while generating minimum spill to interfere with the production lighting.

Boards Contraction of 'switchboard' or 'dimmerboard'. The central control point for the stage lighting. Still the most popular word for a lighting control desk (as in 'What is your board?', 'Where is the board?', 'Who is on the board?', etc) despite the sophistication that has overtaken the simplicity of the original switchboards and dimmerboards. Richard Pilbrow and Strand cleverly hijacked 'Lightboard' as a system name.

Boom Vertical pole, usually of scaffolding diameter, for mounting spotlights. (**Tree** in America.) (*Illus. p. 12.*)

Boom arm Bracket for fixing spotlights to a boom. (**Side Arm** in America.)

Boomerang Manually operated set of filter frames, often four, on a follow spot for rapid colour changing.

Booth Room at the rear of the auditorium, with window to the stage, for control board or follow spots.

Border lights American term for BATTENS.

Borders Strips of neutral or designed material hung above the stage to form an overhead boundary to the scene and to mask the technical regions above the performance area.

Bordoni Bordoni transformers were the standard central European dimmer from the mid-thirties until the late fifties. Each circuit had its own secondary winding which slid in and out of the transformer, moved by a tracker wire from a central control frame with banks of levers. Circuits could accept any load from about 40 watts to 6 kilowatt. These multi-channel autotransformer dimmers never caught on in

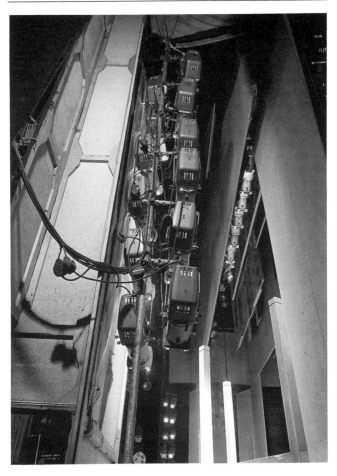

BOOM

Britain except at Glyndebourne where a Bordoni ruled from 1933 to 1963.

Bounce Light reflected from a surface, either accidentally or deliberately.

Bounce cloth See REFLECTOR CLOTH.

Box boom Although originally referring to booms mounted in side wall audience boxes, the term is often used for any side wall lighting in the auditorium, close to the stage. (*Illus. p. 14.*)

Box set A stage setting of an interior location with three walls – ie a complete room with one wall, the 'fourth wall', removed for the audience to see the action. Box sets aim for

BORDONI transformer dimmers

maximum reality in their detailing and many even have a ceiling. Box sets were a reaction against earlier interiors of painted wings and borders; and they have in their turn produced a reaction in favour of more symbolic minimal settings.

Boxed limes Follow spots shuttered to form a rectangle covering the acting area as framed by the proscenium arch. When this rectangle is just head high along the front of the stage to cover the line up for curtain call bows, the term 'stripped limes' is sometimes used. See also LIME BOX.

Bracket handle These boards were the poor cousins of grandmasters. The dimmer handles, which were directly connected to resistance dimmers mounted behind the front panel, could be turned to tighten them on to horizontal

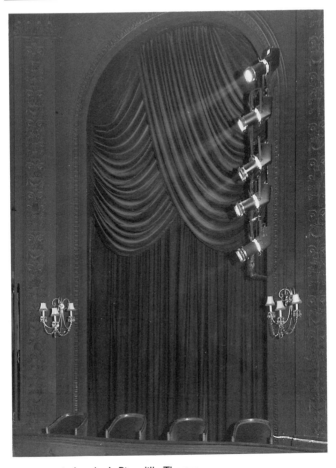

BOX BOOM in London's Piccadilly Theatre

shafts for mechanical mastering. But there was no sophisticated gearing to allow these shafts to move in opposite directions for cross-fading.

Brackets Brackets fixed to walls or ceilings provide very inflexible mounting positions for lighting instruments. Scaffolding bar, accepting hook clamps when horizontal and boom arms when vertical, allows greater choice of position and the possibility of quicker temporary extensions. However brackets screwed to the back of scenery can be useful for mounting small spots.

Brail and breast To pull bars (pipes) upstage or downstage from their natural free-hanging position. In brailing, short rope lines are attached to the ends of the flown bar whereas, in breasting, a rope line is passed across the fly

BRACKET HANDLE Resistance Dimmerboard (Strand)

bar's suspension lines. However the British tend to use the word 'brail', and the Americans 'breast', to cover both methods.

Brecht Bertolt Brecht (1898–1956), German dramatist and director, is a major influence on the philosophy and practice of today's staging. Although often presented as a believer in unfiltered white light, his requirement was for a clarity which he achieved by use of the palest steel blue tinted filters. His lighting style favoured exposed lighting equipment and rejected the use of light for subconscious changes in atmosphere.

Bridges (1) Access catwalks, passing over the stage or incorporated within the auditorium ceiling, usually to facilitate spotlight focusing. (2) Elevators which raise and sink sections of a stage floor.

Broken colour Using two filters in a colour frame, with either or both cut to a pattern or randomly so that the light is filtered by each separately and in combination. This is a particularly effective technique with break-up and foliage gobos. See also POACHED EGG and COMPOSITE GELS.

Bubble Sometimes used as a conversational alternative to 'lamp'.

Build (1) An increase in light intensity. (2) To assemble a scene from its component parts.

Bulb Often used conversationally for lamp – just as lamp is often used for any lighting instrument, whether spot or flood. In America, bulb sometimes refers to the lamp envelope alone.

Bump A sudden increase in light level caused by a build cue with instant timing – ie zero seconds.

Bump in/out Australasian term for the British GET IN/OUT and American **load in/out**.

Bunch light An early flood in which, prior to the availability of high wattage lamps, increased brightness was achieved by mounting several lamps in front of a single reflector.

CAD (Computer Aided Design) See COMPUTERS.

Candela See FOOT CANDLE.

Candles Prior to gas and electricity, stages were lit by candles or oil, often a mixture of both. Candles needed constant attention: their wicks had to be trimmed until the 1820 invention of the plaited wick which, as the candle burned down, curved over into the very hot outer part of the flame where it was consumed. Candles were normally mounted in chandeliers and sconces, but those in the wings were sometimes fixed to poles which could be rotated away from the stage to effect a dim. Electric candles are available to simulate candle light. The standard models (as used, for example, for productions in the eighteenth century Court Theatre at Drottningholm), produce one candlepower of light and have each filament mounted on a spring to produce a slight flicker. More sophisticated types are becoming available with random flickering produced by a microprocessor programmed to simulate all aspects of a flame's performance, including guttering.

Candlepole See POLE.

Cannons Long-range narrow-angle 2kW Lekos.

Cans Headsets comprising one earpiece and boom microphone used for communications between the electrics crew and the stage manager calling the cues. (Plus the lighting designer during rehearsals.)

Carbon See ARCS.

Carousel Although specifically referring to the Kodak series of 35mm slide projectors with circular magazine tray, 'carousel' has become something of a generic term for magazine slide projectors. They are often adapted to use high intensity lamps and are frequently used in banks of several projectors computer controlled through a programme which coordinates the timing of crossfades and slide tray advance.

Cassette (1) Tape cassette memory storage was used in some early control systems, both for intensity and for the positioning of remotely operated spotlights. (2) To speed refocusing during the daily changeover in repertoire theatres, experiments have been made with shutter assemblies in the form of cassettes which can be dropped into the gate. Once their configuration has been determined at the lighting rehearsal, the shutter positions are retained by screws so that daily shuttering becomes as simple as filter changing.

Cat walk An access bridge above the stage or auditorium, but usually referring to one which is narrower than the type of bridge to which lighting instruments are fixed.

C-clamp American clamp for hanging lighting instruments on bars (pipes). See also HOOK CLAMP. (*Illus. p. 18.*)

C-CLAMP

CCT Manufacturing firm who pioneered variable beam profile spots. Their Silhouette and Minuette ranges became standard equipment in the 1970s and 1980s.

C.D. Strand presetting control desk which grew out of the LIGHT CONSOLE. The organ keyboard was replaced by presetting levers but the stopkeys for channel selection remained. These presetting levers were only required to drive the dimmers because inertia took over between moves. Thus the preset could be immediately reset rather than, as in electronic systems, be required to hold the levels between cue moves. This, coupled with the possibility of either manual or piston-memory selection of channels, made the system very flexible and C.D. became the standard board for major British stages and studios from the mid-1950s through much of the 1960s. Its main operational problems were lack of proportional dimming and slowness in 'going back' during rehearsals.

Ceilings Prior to the era of spotlighting, ceilings were a prominent decorative feature of an auditorium, often displaying fine examples of pictorial painting. In the late 1920s and throughout the 1930s, when theatre architecture came under the influence of the cinema, ceilings became a surface to be decorated with soft lighting, usually from sources concealed in coves of art deco fibrous plaster. Today's

Strand c.d. desk for remote operation of a motor driven dimmerbank of resistance and transformer dimmers. Channels to be moved on a particular cue were selected by the organ-style finger tab switches (up to 14 groups could be memorised via the Compton Relay system). The selected channels could be faded up or down as a group or individual levels could be preset. The balanced foot pedal allowed speed to be preset and then adjusted during the progress of the cue.

ceilings tend to be neutral in their decorative finish, and structured to provide lighting positions by incorporating bridges which allow access for maintenance and focusing. On the stage, rooms with ceilings which block overhead lighting bars can be tricky to light. However, the flight from realistic scenery has made such rooms much less common than they were a decade ago.

Century Century Lighting Inc., major innovative New York stage lighting manufacturers founded in 1929 are now part of Strand Lighting. See also KOOK.

Channel A complete control path from the surface operated by the operator's hand, through the processing system, to the dimmer racks. There may be a dimmer dedicated to each channel or the software may allow each dimmer to be programmed (ie soft-patched) to any desired channel.

Channel access Fundamental to the operation of any control system is the method (levers, pushes, keyboard, etc) by which individual channels are brought under operator control. Whether by pulling a large lever or pushing a miniature one or (in the fashion of the current jargon) merely stroking a key, there is need for immediate access to any particular light or groups of lights for on/off and up/down. Access methods used on microprocessor-based boards include light pens pointed at the appropriate data on a video screen and the mouse (qv) which opens up the same scope for the painter's arm as the stopkey (qv) offered to the musician's fingers. However the most popular access remains the keypad. Today's operators were schooled when the pocket calculator re-educated fingers overnight – tomorrow's operators had a Sinclair Spectrum in their prams and write their essays on an Amstrad. Might they feel happier with an alpha-numeric keyboard? Or seek a return to the playability of a lever plus switch-button per lamp/group? Rockboards do, relegating the microprocessor to a facilitating role in effect sequences.

Keypads are the standard means of CHANNEL ACCESS. Tapping the required channel number (eg 36) or group of channels (eg 36+42+43 or 36 thru 39) followed by @ followed by a level (eg 4 for 40%) will move the selected channel(s) to the selected level. The level of selected channel(s) may also be altered by moving the digital encoder wheel up or down.

Channel track A facility, pioneered by Colortran, whereby a specified individual channel's level in every cue can be displayed simultaneously and adjusted. See also TRACKING.

Chase Switching lights, usually by a microprocessor programme, in a looped sequence so that they appear to be 'chasing' each other.

Cheat Moving imperceptibly slowly in the hope that the

audience will not consciously be aware of change. Used particularly for subtle changes in intensity or for repositioning lights .that have been inaccurately focused or subsequently knocked.

Check A decrease in light intensity.

Chiaroscuro Visual texture derived from contrasts of light and shade.

Chief Electrician Senior member of the electrics department. In smaller theatres, responsible for all electrical maintenance of the building in addition to the stage lighting. In larger theatres, deals only with stage lighting while maintenance is handled by a house engineer. In America, called **Master Electrician**.

Choke dimmers See SATURABLE REACTORS. The prospect of an all-electric dimmer, with no moving parts, was always an attractive proposition and the earliest was the simple choke. All chokes, however, have a slow response and the simplest ones require such heavy control currents as to make presetting difficult – or at least the cross-fading between presets that was the unrealised dream of most operators as recently as thirty years ago.

Chopped waveforms Solid state thyristors (and their predecessors, thyratron valves) act as dimmers by chopping the waveform to a greater or lesser degree, letting just as much current pass through as is determined by the controlling signal from the desk.

Choreographer The production team member responsible for devising the movements of dancers (and actors, when applicable).

Chroma A measure of the saturation of a colour – that is, the amount of pure colour within a particular hue.

Chromatic aberration Rainbow coloured rings due to imperfections in lens design and manufacture.

Chromotrope An optical effect where two glass discs, with spiral patterns, rotate in opposite directions to project expanding and contracting images.

CID (Compact Iodide Discharge) A type of high intensity discharge lamp, normally interchangeable with CSI lamps, but offering a light with a colour temperature of 5500°K, approximating more to daylight.

C.I.E. (Commission Internationale de L'Eclairage) A forum for international discussion on all lighting matters. The CIE specialist committee for stage and studio lighting organises occasional conferences and is most widely known for its international symbols for lighting instruments.

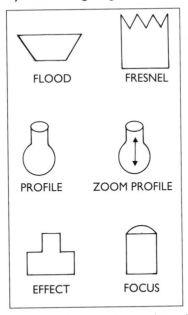

CIE international symbols for some frequently used types of stage lighting instrument.

Cinemoid A self-extinguishing acetate colour filter medium which took over from gelatine which was both fragile and a fire risk. Cinemoid has in turn been superseded by filter materials more able to withstand the high temperatures generated by new light sources and more efficient computer-designed optics. Cinemoid was manufactured in blocks and sliced into thin sheets by a horizontal cutting blade.

Circuit The path from the electrical supply, including dimmer if there is one, to the light. The word circuit is often used loosely to include channel.

Clarity A difficult-to-define quality of light. It is most readily achieved by full intensities and the very palest of tinted filters. The palest blue colour-correcting filters produce more clarity than unfiltered clear light. Saturated colours require very high intensity sources behind them to be even remotely clear, although bold directional statements from a minimum number of angles can also contribute to the clarity of a scene. Muddy light, the opposite of clarity, is produced by a large number of sources dimmed to a level where the redness of the filament is not compensated for by the amount of blue component in the filter.

Cleaners Working lights in the auditorium giving a basic illumination as an alternative to the more decorative house-lights which provide a suitable ambience when an audience is present for performance.

Clémançon Parisian lighting manufacturers founded in 1828 and, until recently, the major force in French lighting technology. During the heady days of lighting's post-war development, Clémançon was led by Georges Leblanc, a man cast in the same necessary mould of enthusiastic committed dictator as Strand's Fred Bentham and Century's Ed Kook. A Leblanc speciality for Clémançon was an electronic device (called 'Chromon' or 'Chromoselector') in which

CLÉMANÇON Jeu d'Orgue with two presets for 60 magnetic amplifier dimmers.

four dimmers were linked to a single pointer to produce a specified colour (calibrated in cinemoid filter numbers) by automatic mixing of red, yellow, green and blue.

Clockwork Moving effects discs were originally powered by clockwork motors which tended to limit their use to accessible positions.

Clouds Realistic or photographic cloud images may be projected from slides. As an alternative, particularly when more symbolic or impressionistic images are required, a gobo projection may be more appropriate. Moving clouds are one of the effects available on motor driven discs for special effects projectors using high output light sources in conjunction with condenser optics to produce an even field of light. Cumulus, storm and fleecy options are available as standard and usually look best when slightly out of focus. Such effects have to be used with considerable care since they can distract the audience's attention away from the

Reiche und Vogel CLOUD Projector (circa 1930)

actors. Cloud projection reached its peak of fashion and technological sophistication in Germany in the 1930s with projectors giving multi-slide images whose trajectory was precisely adjusted with motorised mirrors.

Clutches Electro-magnetic clutches were at the heart of the motor driven dimmer banks. Each dimmer had a pair of clutches (one for up, the other for down) and was moved by the appropriate clutch being energised by a low voltage current from a remote desk.

The motor driven shafts on a Strand remotely operated resistance dimmer bank showing the pairs of electromagnetic CLUTCHES (one for raise, the other for lower) activated from the control desk.

Color American spelling for colour.

Colour The way that coloured light is used in any particular stage production will depend on the style of lighting chosen for that production. It may be that colour is not used at all, or perhaps just a few colour correction (qv) filters added to provide a cool clarity throughout the performance. Perhaps a comedy might be given a slight warming with pink or gold tints for a cheerful enhancement of actors, scenery and costumes. However, the most common use of colour is to establish atmosphere and change it during the progress of the performance. The classic method is to double-cover the acting areas with two sets of spotlights, one coloured happily-warm and the other sadly-cool so that the emotional tone of the scene can be varied in sympathy with the progress of the plot. Like all lighting changes, these may be obvious or subconscious.

Colour call A listing of all the colour filters required in each lighting instrument in the rig.

Colour circle See COLOUR WHEEL (2).

Colour correction filters Video and film cameras are particularly sensitive to the colour temperature (qv) of light sources. Colour correction filters facilitate the matching of different colour temperature sources such as CSI, HMI and tungsten. Although intended primarily for the studio, these filters find use on the stage, particularly for increasing the 'whiteness' of white by adding a touch of palest blue.

Colour magazine A device whereby alternative colour filters may be positioned in front of a spotlight by swinging a

Optional COLOUR MAGAZINE to allow instant changing of six filters on a Teatro Talento follow spot.

chosen frame (usually a choice of 4) either manually, as with a followspot, or remotely using a solenoid or motor. See also AUTOS.

Colour media Another name for colour filters.

Colour mixing Stage lighting involves two possible types of colour mixing: subtractive mixing of filters and additive mixing of light. Since filters remove, by absorption, colours from the spectrum, placing more than one filter in front of a light will result in the removal of extra colours. As more filters are placed in front of the light, more colours will be subtracted until, eventually, no light will pass. Such subtractive mixing offers the possibility of devising special filter combinations if there are no suitable filters available in the standard ranges. But the technique is now used less frequently than it once was, partly because the range of commercial filters is continuously expanding to fill gaps, and partly because more than one in a frame reduces filter life under the heat of the newer sources and more efficient optics. While combining filters in subtractive mixing reduces the light towards black nothing, additive mixing of coloured light moves it increasingly towards white. The three primaries mix to form white as do certain pairs of colours, known as complementaries.

Colour music A performance, without actors, where coloured light changes accompany music in an endeavour to interpret its mood.

Colour temperature A method of measuring the spectral content of 'white' light. The Kelvin scale extends from 2600°K for white light with a red content to 6000°K for white light with a high blue content, with most halogen lamps used in theatre rated at 3200°K. Colour temperature is more critical for the technical eye of a film or video camera than for the human eye.

Colour wheel (1) Filter frames, usually 5, mounted on a wheel which slots into the colour runners of a spotlight. A motor provides continuous rotation or can be fitted with switching for remotely operated colour changing. (2) Diagramatic representation of colours with complementary colours shown as diametrically opposite each other.(*Illus. p. 28.*)

Colouvred lens Black coating baked on to the risers of the steps of a fresnel lens to reduce stray scatter light.

Compact is a word that inevitably lends itself to use as a product name: Strand's 'Compact' board was a compact packaging of the basic units of their Modular Memory

Motorised COLOUR WHEEL for continuous rotation or remote selection of any of the five filters (Strand).

System (MMS). But in the early eighties, shrinking electronics encouraged manufacturers to make some desks so compact that operation became difficult except for those with the slenderest of fingers.

Compact source iodine See CSI.

Company switch American term for a switched and fused supply at the side of the stage for the connection of touring boards. Usually called 'special effects main' in Britain.

Compartment floods Narrow lengths of flooding equipment with lamps wired in two, three or four circuits for colour mixing. Hung above the stage they are known as battens or borderlights, placed on the stage floor they become groundrows – except at the very front when they are footlights or floats.

Complementary colours Pairs of coloured lights which, when added to together, provide white light. For example red and cyan, yellow and blue, green and magenta. Since the filters used in stage lighting are not pure, the light produced by mixing complementary filtered light will get no closer to white than a dirty neutral. See COLOUR MIXING.

Composite gels Two or more filters in a single frame, butt-jointed rather than overlapping. Also called SPLIT COLOUR.

Compton organ console See LIGHT CONSOLE.

Computers Computing technology has been used in stage lighting since the late 1960s when the development of memory facilities for recording intensity levels revolutionised lighting control systems. Microprocessors have made such techniques standard practice. Increasingly sophisticated programmes are being written to assist the management and design of lighting. Starting with customised spreadsheets for managing lighting resources, these now include sophisticated drafting systems with facilities for examining the interacting consequences of instrument position and beam angle selection. See also LIGHTWRIGHT and MODELBOX AUTOLIGHT.

Condenser lens A lens which collects the light from the lamp source in a projector and distributes it evenly across the slide. Also sometimes used in profile spots to produce a smoother light, particularly for following and for gobo projection.

Console Alternative term (now used less than formerly) for the operational desk of a lighting control.

Control surfaces Any device such as lever, push, wheel, rocker, mouse, light pen, cursor, etc, used as an interface between an operator's fingers and the processing system which activates the dimmers or motors controlling lighting instruments.

Cookie An American alternative name for GOBO. A contraction of 'cukaloris', a pattern placed in front of a lighting instrument in film and video to produce a shadow pattern.

Cool Colours in the blue-grey sector of the spectrum (and therefore of relatively high colour temperature) which tend to support a generally depressed atmosphere of sadness. See also WARM.

Correction filters See COLOUR CORRECTION FILTERS.

Count The timing of a cue (by counting) in seconds.

Cove A concealed lighting slot in the auditorium ceiling. In Britain the word tends to be restricted to decorative lighting but in America includes spotlight positions.

Cross-connect American term for panels used in PATCHING.

Cross-fade Lighting change where some of the channels increase in intensity while other channels decrease.

Cross-light Light focused across the stage from one side to the other. Sometimes also used for light focused diagonally.

CSI (Compact Source Iodine) A type of high intensity discharge lamp which is used extensively in follow spots. CSI colour temperature of 4000°K is closer to that of standard stage halogen lamps than either CID or HMI and this makes for easier colour matching.

Cue The signal that initiates a change of any kind. A LIGHTING CUE is a change involving light intensity alterations.

Cue lights Small red (standby) and green (go) lights by which stage managers signal cues to operators. Most cues are now given verbally over an intercom system, with cue lights relegated to a backup role in the event of audio failure. Cue lights are normally wired in series, so that a lamp failure at an outstation will be indicated by the corresponding light on the stage manager's desk also failing to illuminate.

Cue sheet A written operational plot which details timing and actions against each cue number.

Cue synopsis A listing of lighting cues including position in script, duration of change and description of intent.

Curve (dimmer) Much time in the sixties was spent in agonising over which law a dimmer response curve should obey – how the light should change with the movement of the dimmer lever. Most have always been happy enough with the S curve which is produced, so they tell us, by letting a dimmer do what comes naturally – most of the action in the middle, with more gentle change near full and near out. But this is all old hat now that a board's software can allow each dimmer to have its own curve: are there any curve buffs who actually do this? Whatever the curve of the individual dimmers, different cues are likely to require different PROFILES (qv) provided by sensitive accelerations and decelerations of the operator's hand. In advanced systems, this profile can be recorded if required.

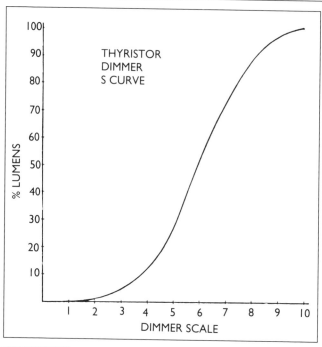

CURVE (DIMMER)

Cut An instant crossfade is a contradiction and so it is called a cut.

Cut-off angle The point in the distribution of light across a beam where the light is less than 1% of its maximum brightness. See LIGHT DISTRIBUTION.

Cyclorama A plain surface, usually cloth, extending around and above the stage to give a feeling of infinite space. The term is often used loosely for any skycloth, either straight or with a limited curve at the ends.

Dance Although facial expression must be visible, body sculpture is the major feature of lighting for dance. Down and across are therefore the main focusing angles, with very few instruments pointing upstage or on a diagonal. The

Dance

staple positions are back and downlights from the overstage bars, with high crosslighting from their ends (known as 'pipe ends') and horizontal crosslighting from towers in the wings. Foh lighting from the auditorium tends to be minimal, particularly in modern dance, and any use of follow spots needs to be particularly discreet if a flattening effect is to be avoided. To provide maximum space for dancing, the stage floor is normally free from raised levels, with scenery positioned only at the sides. This allows the permutations of a large repertoire of short pieces to be dealt with by a permanent rig with standard symmetrical focus, and each dance company tends to develop its own particular version of this.

Dark A theatre temporarily or permanently closed to the public.

Davis Joe Davis (1912–1984) was the major pioneer in establishing the profession of lighting designer in Britain. As a staff member of H.M. Tennent from its inception in 1936, he was responsible for lighting all their productions when, under the leadership of Hugh 'Binkie' Beaumont', they established standards which gave them first refusal of all the best actors, all the best scripts and all the best London theatres. Joe Davis designs were a major contributing factor to theatre's visual quality which he continually fought to raise by battling for more lighting resources and recognition. For some 25 years, Marlene Dietrich would not accept performance engagements unless Joe was available for lighting.

DBO The Dead Blackout which returns all stages to the state from which light brought them hence.

DDM The first major control based on a computer (ie with operational logic derived from a software programme rather than hard-wired circuitry) was DDM named, in the Strand-Bentham tradition, from the initials of an unpublished fuller title – in this case 'Digital Dimmer Memory'. Such systems required a separate computer rack but, within a decade, this was superseded by microprocessor chips mounted within the desk.

Dead (1) The plotted height of a piece of suspended scenery or bar of lights (**trim** in America). (2) Discarded items of scenery.

Dead front Open knife switches and bus bars were mounted on the front of the operational panels of many early dimmerboards. Boards without any live current-

Strand DDM with a rocker switch for each channel. Channel levels were increased or decreased by pressing top or bottom of the appropriate rocker. Internal illumination of the rocker indicated the master and memory status of each channel and touching the central push gave a read out of its level. Memory selection was by numerical columns and there were two playbacks, each with independent control of incoming and outgoing channels.

carrying components exposed to the risk of operator contact were described as 'dead front'.

Deadspot A point on the stage where there is little or no light. Usually unintentional and caused by lack of overlap between adjacent beams.

Delicolour An early form of presetting whereby four resistance dimmers for a 4-colour batten (3 primaries plus white) could be moved mechanically by operation of a single lever to take up the appropriate positions to mix the colour corresponding to a pointer selection of any one of some fifty gel numbers. Invented by Rollo Gillespie Williams. (*Illus. p. 34.*)

Designer (lighting) See LIGHTING DESIGNER.

Designer (scenographer) Responsible for the conception of all visual elements and the supervision of their execution within an agreed budget. Separate designers are often employed for scenery and costumes.

Desk The table from where a seated operator can control the functions of all the stage lighting instruments. Brightness intensity remains the essential control function although,

Furse DELICOLOUR board. The four dimmers for each compartment batten in the rig could be moved simultaneously on cue to the appropriate levels required to produce any colour which had been preset with a pointer calibrated in standard filter numbers.

with developing technology, colour changers, remote positioning and remote focusing are being added to desk facilities.

Diaphragm A plate with a hole of fixed or variable diameter used to control beam width in an optical system. 'Iris diaphragm' is usually contracted to just 'iris'.

Diapositive Transparent positive image for projection – usually called 'slide'.

Dichroic Colour filters which work by reflecting unwanted parts of the spectrum rather than absorbing them in the manner of traditional filters.

Diffuser A filter, often called a frost, which softens a light beam. Used particularly to soften beam edges. See also SILKS.

Digby At the beginning of the twentieth century, the firm of T.J. Digby held a near monopoly of London's West End theatres as a lighting contractor who not only manufactured and supplied the equipment but provided the staff. His lighting technique was based on vast numbers of hand fed carbon arcs (the 'Digby arc') for which a crew of forty men was not unusual.

Digital dimmers Until recently, all dimmers operated on an analogue signal, commonly a voltage of 0 to + or − 10v. Even information originating at the desk in digital form and transmitted as multiplexed (qv) digital signals had to be converted to analogue when it reached the dimmer room. The latest dimmers not only accept digital control signals but most have internal microprocessing which ensures improved stability and self-monitoring, while allowing many optional facilities. Particularly interesting is the possibility of identifying and reporting faults to the control room − especially such previously difficult to trace faults as when a dimmer output is not being accepted because a lamp has blown or plug kicked out.

Digital encoder wheel A control surface with 360° rotation which allows the intensity of a selected channel, group or memory to be increased or decreased. Unlike slider types of lever, wheels have no fixed positions for off or full-on. There is therefore no need to match the control's position to the current memory level before implementing a change. See illustration of CHANNEL ACCESS on p. 20.

Digital logic Virtually all electronic processing of lighting's operational requirements is now carried out digitally with information handled in the form of distinct self-contained bits rather than continuous signals. With the aid of appropriate computer software, data may be handled in any mode which is operationally desirable rather than, as formerly, only in ways which were technically feasible.

Dimensional lighting Lighting from angles which have been chosen to increase the apparent third dimensional depth of actors or elements of scenery to emphasise their sculptural quality.

Dimmers Devices which control the amount of electricity passed to a light and therefore the intensity of that light's brightness. Dimmers distribute and ration each light's electricity in accordance with commands from the operator's fingers − or their hands, knees and elbows in the old days when dimmers of water or wire were under direct manual control. Today's dimmers are solid state devices, usually based on thyristors, receiving their instructions remotely by small currents through multicores or, increasingly, by digital information conveyed through a single wire.

Dimmer bank An assembly of individual mechanical dimmers mounted on a frame.

(Left) Strand EC90 Digital DIMMER RACK.
(Right) Arri Dimmers packaged by White Light in a flight case for touring.

Dimmer rack An assembly of individual electronic dimmers mounted in a cabinet.

Diodes Simple little devices which played a major role in lighting control's electronic revolution. By ensuring that current can only flow in one direction, diodes simplified circuitry generally but, initially and most obviously, they eliminated flicker from grouping switches in the mid-1960s.

Dipless cross-fade When cross-fading from one preset picture to another, it is normally desirable that channels which are common to both remain at the same level without a momentary decrease. Although a commonplace of the new technology, this was once a prime measure of an operator's dexterity.

Dips Small traps in the stage floor giving access to electrical sockets. (**Floor pockets** in America)

Directional diffusers Filters which not only soften the beam but spread it along a chosen axis. Often called 'silks'.

Director Has the ultimate responsibility for the interpretation of the script, controlling the actors directly and controlling everyone else indirectly through the supporting production team (scene, costume, lighting and sound designers, production manager, stage manager etc). Directors should have an ultimate veto but should rarely been seen to exercise such negative power.

Discs Floppy discs are used in lighting control systems as a means of secondary 'library' storage of data for specific productions. The operational programmes are normally stored in integral read-only memories.

Discharge lamps Special high powered light sources utilising an arc enclosed in a gas-filled quartz envelope. It is difficult to dim such lamps with sufficient smoothness for stage use by conventional electrical means. Mechanical shutters are therefore common: this is not a problem with follow spots, but other equipment requires motorised shutters for remote operation. Initial use of discharge lamps was restricted to follow spots and scene projectors but they have become a feature of the new highly sophisticated remote lights such as Vari*Lites.

Dissolve (1) Fading the light on a gauze and building light on the scene behind to make it visible. Sometimes called a

Pani Combi-Color Roller, combining a motorised louvre dimmer shutter and colour scroller in a single unit, fitted to a Quartzcolor Sirio HMI DISCHARGE fresnel spotlight.

bleed. (2) Cross-fading two projected pictures so that one gives way to the other.

Distribution (electricity) The dimmer room is the central point for all electrical distribution concerned with the production lighting. This is where the stage lighting mains supply from the theatre's electrical intake room is switched, fused and passed to the dimmer racks where it is again fused before feeding the socket outlet boxes around the stage and auditorium lighting positions. Patching frames, which were once a dimmer room option (more common in America than in Europe) to be included in the distribution between dimmers and wiring outlets, have now been superseded by soft patching within the desk.

Distribution (light) A spotlight's optical design may choose to place a concentration of intense light at the beam centre, an even light across the beam or somewhere in between. A heap of sand provides a useful analogy in considering the distribution possibilities of the total available light within a beam. Most modern profile spots allow the user to choose an even or peaky distribution when focusing, by including a knob which adjusts the position of the lamp relative to the reflector.

Divertor mirrors See BEAM DIVERTORS.

DMX 512 See PROTOCOL.

Douser American spelling of DOWSER.

Downlight A light focused vertically down – that is, hitting the stage at 90°. Although the most selective lighting angle available to us and very sculptural, downlight does not provide any significant illumination of an actor's face.

Dowser Blackout shutter in a carbon arc spotlight.

Drafting templates See STENCILS.

Drainpipe dimmers See LIQUID DIMMERS.

Drottingholm Swedish theatre on the outskirts of Stockholm, built in 1766. Closed and undisturbed throughout the nineteenth century until rediscovery in 1921 with its machinery, scenery and lights preserved in a cocoon of dust. With the candles in the original floats and wing poles replaced by electric lamps of one candlepower, its productions provide an opportunity to experience the level and quality of eighteenth century theatre lighting.

Dry ice Frozen carbon dioxide dropped into boiling water produces a vapour which is heavier than air and will therefore roll across the stage floor. Dry ice tanks are fitted with immersion heaters, with the more sophisticated models having hinged baskets to lower the dry ice on cue, and fans to direct the vapour which may be led through a wide diameter hose to a convenient emergent point.

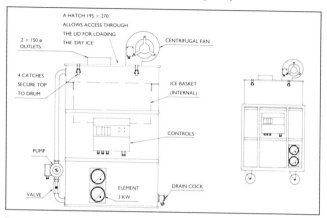

Structure of one of the more sophisticated types of DRY ICE machine (Howard Eaton Lighting). Pump and fan speed are remotely controlled, either directly or through an interface from the lighting board.

Duet Early memory systems required a separate computer rack but, within a decade, microprocessor chips could be mounted within the desks of systems like Duet which made memory a universal facility available to all but the very smallest stages.

Dutch Although Holland is a major theatrical nation with highly sophisticated technology on its stages, there is a long running tendency to use the adjective 'Dutch' for non-orthodox or improvised equipment – such as 'Dutchman' for the condenser lens added to a pc spot to improvise a scene projector.

Earth (**Ground** in America.) The metal case of every lighting instrument must have a direct path to earth to blow the fuse in the event of a fault. All stage wiring is three-cored with live, neutral and earth connections: safety regu-

Earth

lations require all equipment to be designed in such a way that, when the supply is connected, the earth can never be disconnected, not even momentarily during lamp changing.

Effects Many special lighting effects are possible but should always be used as an integral part of the production, never just grafted on 'for effect'. There is nothing quite as effective as a display of moving projections on a cyclorama to distract attention from the actors. See entries on CHASE, CLOUDS, DRY ICE, FIBRE OPTICS, FLAMES, FLICKERS, LASERS, LIGHTING, MAROONS, MIST, PSYCHEDELICS, PYROTECHNICS, RAINBOWS, SMOKE, SNOW, TUBULAR RIPPLES.

Electricity Electricity really has very little to do with lighting – it is just the means by which we process energy today. There was controlled lighting before electricity and the future hopefully holds more sophisticated ways of generating and handling visual waveforms.

Electrics Although lighting personnel are rather more concerned with the light that comes out of an instrument than the electricity which goes into it, lighting technicians tend to be referred to as 'the electrics'.

Electronics This relatively young science has been as big an influence in lighting as it has been in most areas of our lives. The word 'electronic' made its initial major impact on European stage lighting in 1950 with J.T. Wood's Thyratron.

Ellipsoidal Strictly a type of reflector used in many profile spots but extended in America to cover all profile spots.

Ergonomics The science which combines engineering and biology in a search for a sympathetic relationship between people and the design of objects in their environment. Ergonomic design of control systems is particularly concerned with the way in which the various knobs and pushes lie easily under the operator's hand.

ES cap Edison screw cap which allows small wattage lamps to be securely mounted and fed with electricity, particularly in traditional battens and footlights. See also GES and BC.

Extension Short cable used to feed a lighting instrument when its tail is not long enough to reach the desired socket.

Fade Although, strictly speaking, implying only a gradual reduction in brightness, the word *fade* is often used to describe any direction of intensity move – thus *fade-in* and *fade-up*. A *fade-out* takes intensity to zero. See CROSSFADES which can be DIPLESS, SPLIT or PROFILED.

FBO The fade that takes everything to blackout.

False proscenium A scenic portal, particularly one in the downstage area and just upstage of the theatre's structural proscenium. See PORTAL and TORMENTOR.

Fibre optics The smallest pin points of light used on the stage are the ends of optical fibres. These may be terminated through tiny holes in scenery. Individual fibres are harnessed together and clamped to a special spotlight with a motorised colour wheel which can produce positive colour changes – or just twinkling when the points of light are used as stars on a black sky cloth. (*Illus. p. 42.*)

Field angle More formally known as the 'one-tenth peak angle'. The point in the distribution of a light beam where the intensity falls away to a tenth of its peak value.

Filament image Poor optical design or inferior lenses and reflectors in a spotlight can result in an image of the lamp filament being projected under some combinations of focus and throw. This is, however, unlikely with modern equipment.

Filament striation A linear unevenness in the beam usually resulting from poor centering in the optical system of the lamp and, therefore, its filament.

Fill Soft light, generally from the front, may be used to blend areas and smooth out any undesirable hardness or shadows. Such fill light may also be used for subtle colour toning.

Filter Material placed in front of an instrument to colour or diffuse the beam. Traditional filters absorb the unwanted wavelengths of the spectrum while dichroic filters reflect them. Because of the fire risk, filters are no longer made from gelatine but from polyester or polycarbonate film with

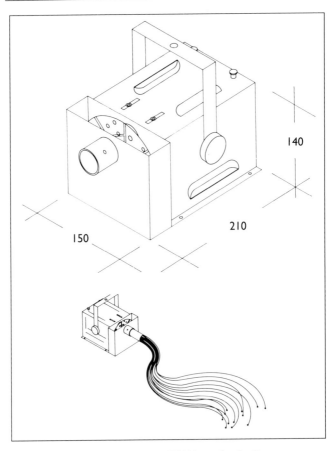

Compact light source, using a 12v 50W lamp, for feeding a FIBRE OPTIC harness (Howard Eaton Lighting).

the dyes incorporated within the material applied to the surface or sandwiched between two layers.

First electric An American term for the first lighting bar upstage of the proscenium. The British equivalent term is 'number one spot bar'.

Fixture A word sometimes used as an alternative to 'instrument' or 'lantern'. Also used for practical light fittings (wall brackets, chandeliers, etc) and there has been some tendency, particularly by manufacturers, to refer to the new computerised moving lights as 'automated fixtures'.

Flag A piece of matt black metal (not unlike a single barndoor leaf), mounted in front of a spotlight to cut-off stray light falling in a particular direction. Often mounted by a multi-jointed arm clamped to the fork (trunnion) of the spotlight, when it is usually called a 'French flag'.

Flame effects A moving image of flames may be projected from an optical effects disc (see EFFECTS). Flame shaped gobos in the gate of profile spots may be given an illusion of movement by use of a rotating disc (often called a 'kk wheel') mounted in front of the lens. However it is often more effective to show the light reflected by fire – ie by a shimmering mix of red and amber. For this, break-up gobos with a kk wheel may be used; and there is a rotary disc with break-up glass available to fit older Strand fresnels. (With a change of colour filter, this effect is very good for the shimmering light reflected off water.)

Flare Unwanted light which is reflected from scenery or from parts of spotlights in front of their lenses, such as barndoors.

Flash (1) Momentary switching a light on and off. Some control desks, especially those designed for rock and pop music productions, have a manual flash button associated with each channel fader. Channels can be programmed to flash at random or in planned sequences at predetermined time intervals. (2) The detonation of a pyrotechnic device.

Flash box Small box holding a pyrotechnic powder charge which explodes when detonated electrically. In the older types, a piece of wire was stretched between two terminals and covered with a teaspoonful of powder which ignited when current was passed to melt the fuse wire. More modern devices use measured charges of powder pre-loaded in enclosed capsules which plug into a socket in the flash box.

Flash out A check to discover whether lights are working, and plugged correctly, by switching them on one at a time.

Flicker Increasing and decreasing a light's intensity very rapidly – so fast that it is best done by a microprocessor. See also STROBE.

Flicker wheel Disc with narrow slots rotated in front of a light, particularly a follow spot or effects projector, to make the light flicker. Called **Lobsterscope** in America.

Floats Jargon for footlights. Originates from an era when, prior to the development of Argand lamps, wicks floated in an oil reservoir.

Float spot Originally a small spotlight tucked into the footlights, but now used for any floor-level spotlight mounted at the front of the stage.

Flood (1) A simple instrument, without a lens, giving fixed spread of light. (2) To adjust any lighting instrument to enlarge the beam in order to cover a wider area with light.

Traditional FLOOD.

Floor pocket American term for DIPS.

Floppy disc See DISC.

Flys The area above the stage into which scenery can be lifted out of sight of the audience

Focal length The distance between a lens and its focal point.

Focal point Rays of light falling on a lens, parallel to its axis, are refracted (bent) to converge at a focal point of the lens.

Focus spots Simple spotlights where lamp and reflector move together in relation to a fixed plano-convex lens. The latest type use a prism-convex lens to overcome some of the beam quality problems inherent in a clear plano-convex lens.

Focusing Strictly speaking, focusing is the adjustment of lights to give a clearly defined image. But the term is normally used to cover the whole process of adjusting the direction and beam of spotlights in which the desired image may be anything but clearly defined.

Fog See SMOKE for the machines which precipitate mist and fog in the atmosphere. The presence of fog may also be indicated by hanging gauze screens on the exterior of windows.

FOH All instruments which are 'front of house', ie on the audience side of the proscenium.

FOH inhibitor See INHIBITORS.

Follow on A lighting change which does not have a sig-nalled start point but commences immediately after the conclusion of the previous cue.

Follow spot Spotlight with which an operator follows actors around the stage. They are normally either profiles or beamlights. Followspotting may be discreetly soft-edged and balanced within the general light. Or it may be obtrusively hard-edged and obvious to the extent that it is more a statement about star status than a mere source of illumination.

Foot candle Unit of measurement of illumination based on the light produced by a candle at a distance of one foot. This is identical with measurements expressed as lumens per square foot. Since a candle provides a somewhat crude, although surprisingly accurate, standard measure for an age of high technology, it has been replaced by a source produc-ing a candela which for practical purposes can be regarded as identical.

Footlights Long strips of flooding equipment along the front of the stage arranged in 3 or 4 circuits for colour mixing. (*Illus. p. 46.*)

Foot pushes The foot is a much underused portion of a board operator's anatomy. In Bentham's console and C.D., foot pushes were used as operational switches, usually doub-ling up the function of certain finger pushes primarily to free the hands for other tasks at critical moments. This might be

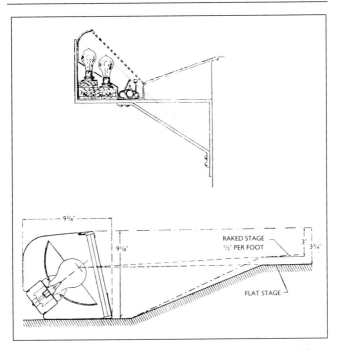

(A) Early electric FOOTLIGHT with coloured lamps and gaslight in reserve.

(B) Later compartmented FOOTLIGHT for use with filters.

thought to be a rather specialised technique appealing to organists, but the balanced pedal for speed regulation is a very natural movement for any driver, especially since sensitive board operation requires subtle acceleration and deceleration rather than a uniform speed maintained throughout the cue.

Fortuny Mariano Fortuny (1871–1949), the Spanish fabric designer, pioneered the fully domed cyclorama which he lit with coloured silk filters.

Fork Sometimes called 'trunnion arm'. The stirrup within which the body of a lighting instrument hangs and tilts.

Forward perch Term coined by Joe Davis for side lighting positions in the auditorium but very close to the proscenium.

Four wall rental A type of rental agreement, common in London's West End and New York's Broadway, where all lighting equipment (and staff in New York) is provided and installed by the renting production company.

Frame Rectangle, usually metal but sometimes card, which supports a colour filter inserted into the runners on the front of an instrument.

French flag See FLAG.

Fresnel spot Spotlight which gives a soft-edged light due to its fresnel lens which has a stepped moulding on the front and a textured surface on the back.

Frontcloths (1) Scenic cloths hanging at the front of the stage. (2) Variety acts who can perform in the shallow depth of stage in front of a frontcloth.

Frost A diffuser (qv) filter used to soften a light beam.

FUF (Full-up-finish) An increase to bright light over the last couple of bars of a musical number.

Fuse Protective device, either cartridge or piece of special wire, which melts when its rated electrical current is exceeded. All parts of a control system are protected by fuses: for the power circuits they are located in the dimmer room and for the electronics at the desk. Cartridges have mostly superseded wire, although circuit breakers on dimmers are common practice in America. In countries where the voltage is 240/220 rather than 120/110, circuit breakers are still relatively rare in the dimmer room: there tends to be too fine a balance between a breaker that is sensitive enough to protect the dimmer and yet not oversensitive to minor electrical surges.

Gas Gas lighting was introduced into theatres in the early nineteenth century and became the main source of stage lighting for most of that century, especially in the metropolitan theatres. The new brightness was not universally admired, giving rise to unfavourable comparison with the delicate atmospheric light of oil and candles. (Similar arguments were heard when electricity supplanted gas.) Gas brought lighting, for the first time, under control from a central point and, although much of the equipment was flooding, with battens above the stage and footlights at the front, the limelight introduced spotlighting which became

THE LIGHTS O' LONDON.

GAS AND LIME LIGHT.

ACT I.

Full up to commence.   Full Set.
White lengths and ground-rows at every avail-
    able place, full up to commence.
Green lengths and ground-rows at every avail-
    able place, turned right down to commence.
Lamp over gate to light.
3 White Limes from L. H. to flood stage at
    cue————poor all my life.
1st check to Gas.
Change White Limes to Yellow.
    ————good luck go with you.
2nd check to Gas.
Change Yellow Limes to Red.
        ————I wish to see your face no more.
3rd check to Gas.
Turn off Red Limes.
Gradually turn up green floats, lengths, and
    ground-rows.
        ————God knows when we shall meet
                again.
Turn on Green Limes for moonlight

ACT II.

Sc. 1.— Full up.   2
    2 lengths outside window in R.F.
    1 length outside bar L.H.
    Fire burning on hearth R.H.
    Red Lime through ditto.

Sc. 2.— Checked.   Full Set.
    Green floats and green mediums.
    Green lengths at every available place.
    3 Green Limes from L.H. to flood stage.

Lighting plot for a touring show in the GAS era.

very sophisticated in the spectacular productions of London's West End.

Gas tables can be considered the first really centralised lighting controls (but see CANDLEPOLE). Centralised location of the gas taps allowed individual lighting instruments to be faded, and there was a system of pilot jets to permit circuits which had been faded out to be rekindled remotely.

Gate The optical centre of a profile spot where the shutters are positioned and where an iris or gobo can be inserted.

Gauze Fabric which becomes transparent or solid under appropriate lighting conditions (**Scrim** in North America).

GAS TABLE

GES cap 'Goliath Edison Screw' cap used on larger wattage general service lamps, particularly those in older 1 kW floods. **Mogul screw base** in America.

Gel Still used as a general term for colour filters although gelatine media were phased out in the middle of the present century. The inflammability of gelatine filters made them an unacceptable fire hazard. They quickly faded and became brittle, even with older cooler lamps.

Get in Unloading a production into the theatre. **Load in** in America. **Bump in** in Australasia.

Get out (1) Dismantling a production and loading it on to transport for removal from the theatre. **Load out** in America. **Bump out** in Australasia. (2) The minimum weekly box office receipts that will cover the production expenses to the point of breaking even.

Ghost load American term for an extra lamp plugged to a resistance dimmer to match the connected load to that dimmer's rating for a smooth fade. See LOADS and RATING.

Glare A light which is too bright and/or too harsh for comfort. The commonest cause is uncontrolled reflections.

Glyndebourne has always been in the forefront of lighting technology. The opera house opened in 1934 with a Bordoni board offering load independence from 5W to 5kW on each channel, and there were 40 presettable 'stops' on each channel's control lever. Such load flexibility did not become general in Britain until after 1964 – by which time Glyndebourne had become the first theatre in Europe to install thyristors; and a control desk whose functions could be temporarily duplicated in mid-auditorium for rehearsal.

Gobo A mask placed at the gate of a profile spotlight for simple outline projection. Also used, with softened focus, to texture the beam.

Gobo holders Home-made gobos are usually cut to the correct width to fit the gate runners of a specific profile spot. Commercial gobos, however, are made in three standard sizes to fit a wide range of gobo holders. The gobo may be rotated in the holder, but orientation is much easier and quicker when the spotlight has a rotatable gate.

Gobo rotators Rotators, with variable speed reversible motors, fitting into the slot provided for a drop-in iris at the gate of profile spots. See also ANIMATION DISCS.

Grandmaster (1) The summit of the application of pure mechanical engineering to lighting control. Individual dimmer handles could be locked to horizontal shafts, each of

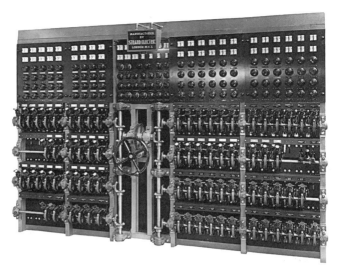

which could be selected to raise or lower when the single master wheel was turned on cue. All done by gears. Grandmasters were well suited to the variety stage's washes of coloured flood lighting from battens, floats and wing floods – with the red, blue, amber and white dimmers each having their own shafts. Spotlight rigs were more complex to operate, particularly for plays. But in many theatres, particularly the number one touring houses, there were teams (often, of not more than two people for 96 dimmers) who could perform feats of the most incredible dexterity. With enough operators (ie a lot) everything was possible, including some cues that can still be difficult on even the most sophisticated of today's computer boards. (2) A fader that masters the output of an entire preset board, including preset masters, submasters, group masters, etc.

Graph plot A plot which provides a record of the focus details of each instrument and its intensity level in each cue. Information is displayed in columns for easier reference than is possible with a plot prepared for working a board during performance. Graph plots can be generated automatically by the more sophisticated computer boards and, if desired, it is possible to arrange software so that a board may be programmed from a graph plot.

Grelco Moulded splitter with a single 15 amp 3-pin plug feeding two integral 15 amp 3-pin sockets.

Grid The arrangement of wooden or metal slats on which the pulley blocks of flying systems are mounted.

Ground An alternative term for EARTH, particularly in America.

Groundrow (1) A low piece of scenery standing on the stage floor. (2) Lengths of compartmented lighting floods placed on the stage floor.

Grouping A subdivision, temporary or permanent, of the channels in a control system – with each group subject to its own submaster. The formation of channels into groups has always been one of the more contentious areas of board design. It was certainly the major point of debate in the design of the manual preset desks which accompanied the thyristor revolution in the mid-sixties. Bentham was convinced that the groups should be common across all presets: most users favoured the possibility of forming different groups within each preset. Thus 'SP' boards had a single set of grouping switches while 'Threeset' had a set of switches for each preset. The most versatile boards were the 'LP' and its more sophisticated progeny 'Lightset' which probably had just about the most flexible grouping achievable without a computer. The Strand grouping tradition, followed by Thorn on their introduction of pin patch, allowed flexible grouping whereas the repertoire tradition of central Europe tended to breed a system of fixed groups corresponding to the geographical layout of the installation. Development of memory controls has involved a growth in the number and flexibility of group masters. The launch of the first viable memory system included quite an intense discussion on whether or not groups would now be redundant (the pro-totype had none) – and the grouping debate still continues, particularly between those requiring a board for formally plotted shows and those wishing to create instant lighting during performance.

Half A convenient plotting level when boards were either uncalibrated or their operational procedures made the use of such basic calibrations as 1 to 10 unrealistic. 'Full', 'three-quarters', 'half', 'quarter' and 'out' provided the usual scale with 'plus' or 'minus' added sparingly and optimistically.

Half-peak angle The point in the distribution of a light beam where the intensity falls away to half of its peak value. The eye perceives peak to half-peak light as a virtually even beam.

Halogen The halogen gas introduced into tungsten lamps from the 1970s has had a marked influence on the manage-ment and quality of stage lighting. Extended life has dramati-cally reduced the number of occasions on which lights 'blow' in the middle of rehearsal or performance. But most import-ant is the maintenance of full light output throughout life. Whereas tungsten lamp filaments deposited particles on the inside of the glass envelope, causing gradual blackening, the halogen gas cycle returns these particles to the filament, keeping the glass clear. Halogen lamps run very hot and have to be handled with extreme care. The quartz envelopes are very sensitive to grease or moisture and the special glove supplied with each new lamp should always be used when inserting into a spotlight.

Hamburg A subtle Rosco diffuser (114) also available in half (119) and quarter (164) strengths. Although, strictly speaking, a Rosco product name, Hamburg frosts are tending to become a generic name for the newer series of delicate filters which allow PC spots to be progressively softened (making fresnels obsolescent) and allowing profiles to be soft-edged without defocusing the lenses.

Hat Short black metal tube added to the front of a spot-light to control spill and (particularly when used with side foh) limit audience distraction by masking lens and colour frame.

Highest takes precedence When several presets have their masters at full, the dimmer level of any channel which is alive on more than one preset is the highest individual setting of that channel. This is standard system philosophy for all preset controls.

Hire See RENTAL.

HMI (Hygerium Metalic Iodide) A type of high intensity discharge lamp used mainly in scenic projection and follow spots. As with other discharge sources, HMI is not normally dimmed electrically for stage use, due to difficulties in achieving a sufficiently smooth electrical dim, particularly when approaching zero light.

Hook clamp A clamp for hanging an instrument from a horizontal bar, usually of scaffolding diameter.

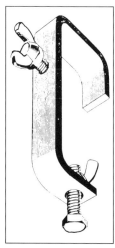

HOOK CLAMP

Hook up American term for a plot which lists, against each dimmer number, the instruments connected to it plus their focus and colour.

Holophane The name of a company and their product which automatically mixed primaries when a pointer was moved to a particular colour name. See also DELICOLOUR.

Horizon German for sky cloth and consequently used as a name for cyclorama floods, particularly an older type of wide angle cylindrical flood with a long linear filament 1kW tungsten lamp.

Hot spot (1) The brightest part of the light of a spotlight which has been adjusted to have a peaky beam (see DISTRIBUTION). (2) A position on the stage which is particularly bright due to uneven focusing or balancing.

House board A theatre's permanent control is called the house board when another board is brought in temporarily by a touring company.

Houselights The decorative lighting in the auditorium.

Hue General classification of colours in terms of their spectral names: red, yellow, orange, blue, magenta, etc.

Hydraulic Hydraulic power was used to operate dimmers at the Royal College of Music in a lighting installation which was away ahead of its time in many respects, not only at its inauguration in 1925 but for many years after. Indeed the capability for a single operator to control so many dimmers moving at independent speeds was not achieved again until the computer age. Each channel had a hydraulic valve which set its dimmer travel at any required rate up to thirty minutes.

IDM Having led the field in the 1960s in developing a memory board with digital logic, called *IDM/R* (Instant Dimmer Memory/Rocker), Strand Electric (as they then were) took a decision which must have been based on marketing rather than technical grounds. They attempted a lever-per-channel board called *IDM/L* (Instant Dimmer Memory/Lever) which provided an exciting ride for its users, even when the drum memory was whizzing sweetly and the crates of analogue to digital converters were finely trimmed. Moreover an interpretation of fail safe as 'all channels to full' might have been safe for TV but could be disastrous in a theatre, both for the show and for the maximum demand electricity tarrif.

Illumination Whereas the use of light for such matters as creating atmosphere or defining areas may be optional, illumination to provide sculptural visibility is at the core of every stage lighting design. The amount of light required is neither definable nor measurable: brightness is relative rather than absolute. It depends upon balance, with the brightest point on the stage setting a contrast scale to which the eye relates everything. The amount of light required is also related to the activities of the muscular iris in the human eye which opens or closes in response to light level. The iris tends to react slower than a fast lighting cue and lighting designers need to take into account not just the balance within a scene but that scene in relation to previous and following cues.

Incandescent lamp A wire filament, enclosed with a gas (originally a vacuum) within a glass envelope, which emits light when an electric current is passed through.

Independents were originally the circuits that did not conform to the colour wash groupings which were the basis of the horizontal shaft layout of the levers of most directly operated boards. In the more sophisticated of these boards, any circuit could be switched to be 'independent' of the main blackout contactors. Grouping in early all-electric boards often consisted of a three-way switch offering off/ main master/independent master. Today's independents are non-dimmable channels (increasingly called 'non-dims'), not subject to the board's dimming and mastering networks, although their on/off switches may be mounted on the same control desk.

Indirect light Light which is transmitted via reflection rather than arriving straight from its source.

Inertia Dimmer inertia was a feature of electro-mechanical systems (see LIGHT CONSOLE and C.D.). Once dimmers had been moved, they held that level until told to move again (even if the control cable from desk to dimmers was cut) whereas all-electric presetting of thyristor dimmers requires a current to be always present to hold a dimmer at its level. However, the computer logic of memory boards can simulate inertia with thyristor dimmers so that the operator need only be concerned with channels which move on cue.

Infinite presetting The memory revolution introduced the possibility of infinite presetting whereby it is possible to include enough memory capacity to place no limit on the number of scenes that can be preset for a performance – and even for a repertoire season.

Inhibitors Master faders which prevent selected groups from becoming alive. The most common is an 'foh inhibitor' which offers immediate override control of all light sources on the auditorium side of the house curtain, independently of their status on any of the other masters.

Instrument A stage lighting unit such as a spotlight or flood. An American term coming into increasing international use. See also LANTERN and LUMINAIRE.

Intake Not a reference to the lighting crew's capacity for refreshment but the room where the electricity supply enters the building and is metered, switched and fused.

Integral dimmers Although dimmers are normally located in a central dimmer room, and occasionally in racks adjacent to particular geographical sections of the installation, it is possible that developing technology may find it more convenient to place the dimmer within the spotlight. The light would receive power from a ring supply, and digital instructions from a control loop. The idea becomes particularly attractive when control signals are also being supplied for such other functions as remote movements and colour change. Heat dissipation seems likely to remain the major problem.

Intelligent lights Sometimes used to describe remotely operated computer controlled instruments. However, as such lights do not think for themselves but perform precisely as instructed, perhaps 'obedient lights' would be a more accurate term.

Intensity The brightness of each lighting instrument, balanced to make a lighting picture. Intensity control is the fundamental purpose of any lighting board.

Inverse square law Light intensity is inversely proportional to the square of the throw distance between a light and the object lit. That is, doubling the throw distance reduces the light to a quarter.

Iris (eye) The muscle-operated diaphragm in the human eye which adjusts the eye's aperture to changing light intensities.

Iris (spotlight) An adjustable circular diaphragm which alters the gate size in a profile spot.

Iris out A way of ending a song where a slow fade to blackout of the stage lighting is lagged by a tightening of the iris of a follow spot so that the light is gradually concentrated on the singer's face before going out with the last note. This process requires very sensitive timing. In certain circumstances an iris out may be followed by a return to bright light for the singer to acknowledge applause.

Isora A plastic skycloth, lit from behind.

Izenour George Izenour (b.1912) pioneered electronic lighting control in the USA, particularly multipresetting in association with various types of dimmers. Izenour was also involved in many aspects of stage engineering and later became a theatre consultant whose auditoria are noted for purity of sightline as their major priority.

Jacks (and Jills) Manual patching often used Jack plugs and sockets. These sockets were sometimes called Jills. (Patching became microprocessed around the time that such terminology became sensitive to allegations of sexism.)

Joystick A control lever which can be simultaneously moved to the left or right while moving forward and backward. It was tried experimentally in the 1930s for three-colour mixing and as a master on one of the prototype Strand 'Compact' desks (Compact was a basic package of MMS modules). Joysticks have been mooted as a possibility for remote movement control of spotlights. (*Illus. p. 58.*)

J.P. Junior Preset was the first European board to make the joys of thyristor dimming available to a mass market. Coded J.P./2 or J.P./3 according to a number of presets, each preset had a rotary knob master and there were no grouping facilities.

J.P.

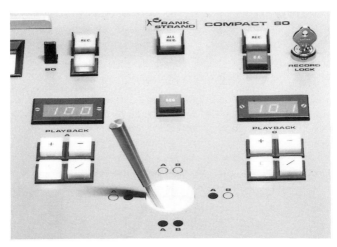

A prototype JOYSTICK master (Strand Compact). Up/down movement gave a dipless crossfade, while lateral movement offered optional lead or lag of the incoming memory.

Strand JUNIOR 8 resistance board.

Junior 8 The climax of low cost, but high quality and reliable resistance dimming. Eight circuits were paired to four dimmers with each circuit having a three-way switch offering off or through dimmer or independently full. The dimmers, switches, fuses, sockets and master blackout were integrally mounted in a unit which could be carried easily by one person. Plotting and operating probably required a higher degree of concentration than any board before or since.

Kelvin A scale for measuring the whiteness of light, the normal range of halogen lamps being between 3000°K and 3400°K. See COLOUR TEMPERATURE.

Keyboard The method of access to channels and memories most frequently used on control boards is the keypad layout of the pocket calculator. Although the alpha-numeric keyboard (the 'qwerty' layout of the typewriter and personal computer) can and has been used for access, its inclusion in a control desk is more usually for the input of auxilliary information about the nature of cues as a useful aide-mémoire on the system's VDU screen.

Keylight A light which makes a positive visual statement about the main light source within a scene – particularly its direction.

Keystone The distortion of shape when a projected image hits a surface at any other angle than straight on 90°.

Kill A poetically incisive command for 'switch off'.

Kilowatt See WATTAGE.

Kinetics Light may be passively constant throughout a performance but kinetic changes can provide the stage environment with an optional fourth dimension of time, with the scale of changes varying from imperceptibly slow crossfades to computer programmed sequencing and wildly gyrating moving lights.

KK wheel Rotating perforated wheel mounted in the colour runners of a profile spot to induce an illusion of movement in a gobo's pattern.

Kliegl One of the great pioneers of American lighting manufacturing firms, founded in 1896. (In 1974, Kliegl directors still referred to their desks as their 'benches'.)

Kook Edward F. Kook (1903–1990). Ed Kook of Century Inc. was the Runyonesque New Yorker who animated American lighting technology during its critical growth phase.

Ladders Framework in the shape of a ladder (but not climbable) for hanging side lighting.

Lamp The light source within an instrument, although sometimes used as an alternative to the word instrument.

Lamp check A pre-rehearsal or pre-performance check to ensure that no lamps have blown or instruments been knocked. Normally a memory file number is allocated so that all rigged equipment can be brought easily to a low level for this check.

Lamp dip In the days when exposed lamps were used in battens, footlights and lengths, the lamps were coloured by dipping, usually when hot, in a special lacquer. For the occasional colouring of lamps today, FEV (French Enamel Varnish) is used.

Lantern A luminaire designed or adapted for stage use. A traditional word now being overtaken by the American INSTRUMENT.

Lasers (Acronym for Light Amplification by Stimulated Emission of Radiation.) Laser technology, particularly the production of holograms, may hold exciting future prospects for scenography. Currently, their main contribution to performance is the three dimensional images produced by the laser beam's intensity and speed which leaves a trace hovering in space. This requires no screen other than some smoke in the air plus careful balancing of the other light. Laser light has a unique luminous quality, generating particularly effective dynamic wave patterns, such as undulations and perspective tunnels.

Layout A lighting plan, with its associated section(s), is often referred to as a lighting layout. These documents, usually scaled at 1:25, or less frequently 1:50, show the instruments to be used, their positions, filters, accessories and channel numbers.

Leko American term (shortened from the brand name Lekolite, derived from the names of its inventors, Levy and Kook) for an ellipsoidal profile spot manufactured by Century (now part of Strand Lighting). Use often extended to all makes of ellipsoidal, so that it has, in effect, become a generic term.

Strand LEKO

Lengths Lampholders screwed to timber battens were once hung behind scenery flats to light door backings etc. Every theatre had a collection of assorted lengths of 'length', but their use died out during the 1950s.

Lenses The lenses commonly used in stage spotlights are plano-convex or fresnel. Clear plano-convex lenses (flat on one side and convex on the other) are used singly or in combinations for profile spots. Plano-convex lenses with a crystalline texture on the piano surface are used in simple focus spots, with fresnels as an alternative when a particularly soft light is required. See also OBJECTIVE LENS.

Lens tube For focusing purposes, the lenses of profile spots were mounted, traditionally, in a tube which slid backwards and forwards within another tube attached to lamphouse. Such an arrangement, however, is prone to jamming if the outer tube receives even the slightest dent. Consequently, in most modern spotlights the lenses travel on a rack system within the spotlight's outer casing.

Level The intensity of a light is often referred to as its level.

Levers are the traditional means of controlling channel intensity on manual boards – a pushing and pulling action which became miniaturised with electronics. The old 'beer pump' lever gave a physical satisfaction that cannot quite be equalled by a miniature fader. And certainly not by a button. Now button pushing has been replaced by key stroking: hardly physical, but potentially sensual.

Library storage Modern control systems usually have more than enough memory capacity to retain all data for even the most complex production. However it is normal practice to offload this information into a secondary storage, usually floppy disc. It is then a quick and simple matter to load the appropriate production into the system for a particular performance.

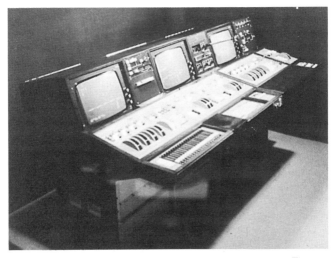

Strand LIGHTBOARD as installed for the opening of the National Theatre in London.

Lightboard is the ultimate in board naming and Richard Pilbrow bestowed it upon the National Theatre system which he devised with Strand in the mid-70s and which became the standard in several major international theatres, taking over the slot of DDM. From Lightboard onwards, video displays and flexibility in forming groups became an indispensable feature of every board.

Light box To light sections of translucent scenery from behind, lamps may be mounted in a shallow box fixed to the back of the scenery with pin hinges. The box prevents unwanted light spill, protects the lamps and may be fitted with reflective material and/or faced with diffuser filter to improve performance.

Light centre length Distance between the centre of a lamp's filament and a standard point in its base.

L.C. Being a choke dimmer, one might assume that the L and C in L.C. stood for inductance and capacitance, but they were for Len's Choke. Designed by Len Leggett, this was Strand's downmarket response to the magnetic amplifier which, prior to the thyristor, dominated everywhere in Europe except Britain. L.C. had a small transistor amplifier which reduced the control current to practicable levels for presetting. The choke was, inevitably, so slow in acting that all channels had separate relay switching for blackouts. (Too hasty a return after blackout produced a momentary picture of the previous state – an early, if undesirable, manifestation of memory!)

Light console Fred Bentham was the first to bring control of a large lighting installation under the fingers of a single operator. He adapted the console of a Compton organ using the stopkeys to select channels for movement, and the keyboard to move the dimmers by motors on a remotely located dimmer bank. Speed was determined by the operator's foot on a pedal. Movement continued for as long as the operator's fingers pressed the keys and so considerable dexterity was required to 'drop off' individual dimmers at levels other than full or out. Selection of groups of channels to move was simplified by deploying the Compton organ's piston memory. The light console was at its best for musicals involving bold fades, cuts and flashes rather than finely balanced levels. It had an operational flexibility, particularly for instant lighting, which was not repeated until the development, of ROCKBOARDS. The level difficulty was solved in the 1950s by fitting polarised relays to the clutches through which the single motor drove the individual dimmers. These

Strand-Bentham LIGHT CONSOLE at the London Coliseum.

boards were at first called CONSOLE PRESET but became established as System C.D.

Light curtain A 'curtain' or 'wall' of light produced by a row of intense PAR lamps at close centres. The resultant haze tends to obscure the scene behind but, like all effects dependent upon light bouncing off dust particles in the air, it is helped by the presence of a little smoke. Success is also assisted by a non-reflective floor and a slight backlighting angle to throw any floor reflections forward. Most light curtains use low voltage lamps wired in series to enable them to run directly from a mains voltage dimmer. Wiring may be alternate, as with battens, to allow colour mixing; or a colour scroller may be fitted.

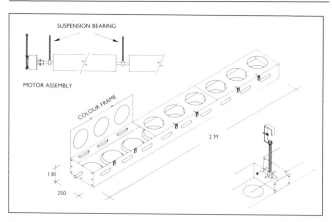

Structure of a LIGHT CURTAIN with motor for remote control of angle. (Howard Eaton Lighting).

Light entertainment This is not an entertainment based on light (but see COLOUR MUSIC). It is a broad spectrum of theatre covering all manner of stagings from unrelated sequences of free-standing variety 'acts' to spectacular revues with star personality performances in a framework of lavish production numbers. Variety performers have self-contained acts complete with lighting requirements which designers working in light entertainment have to interpret. These plots are still frequently written in the language of the three-coloured batten rigs of the old variety theatres, but such terms as 'full-up', 'red stage', 'blue stage', 'colours', 'blackout' or 'iris out', give all the necessary indications of the lighting mechanics of an act and its atmosphere sequence.

Lighting designer The member of the production team responsible for the conception and execution of the lighting within agreed budgets and schedules. Lighting designers determine the lighting style in consultation with the director and design team, plan an appropriate equipment rig and supervise its installation and focusing. They compose the lighting plot at the lighting rehearsals and supervise its execution and modification throughout the dress rehearsals.

Lighting director A term with no clearly defined standard usage, but generally implying a wide responsibility for many aspects of a theatre's lighting department including resource management in addition to design.

Lighting manager Usually employed by repertoire theatres to take responsibility for supervising changeovers and maintaining standards, particularly of productions lit by visiting freelance designers.

Light leaks (1) Unwanted light from a spotlight casing, probably through poorly designed ventilation. (2) Light visible through joins between sections of the scenery or through its material. Cured by stripping the joins and either painting the back of the canvas or hanging neutral material.

Lightning Lightning has two basic forms – *sheet* and *fork*. Sheet lightning is a rapid series of all-over short intense bursts and care has to be taken that this all embracing light does not show up such stage mechanics as the masking, especially borders and the shadows they may throw. For this reason it is often better, if the format of the scene allows, to position the lightning source at stage level, possibly at the bottom of the sky, rather than above the stage. If directed from front, above or sides, careful shuttering is essential. Normal lamp filaments have too slow a rise and decay time so, while simple sheet lightning may be generated from special photographic lamps such as the photoflood, electronic devices are required for credible high intensity flashing. Forked lightning can be projected in slide or gobo form: the intensity requires discharge type lamps and lightning's irregular flashes are most readily produced by an operator using a simple hand-operated blackout card in front of the lens. The presence of an operator allows the placing of the fork image to be changed between bursts and this is a major aid to credibility. However the latest fast acting mechanical shutters can be programmed as required and sophisticated strobe pulsing programmes are available.

Light palette This evocative name for what a board is supposed to provide was adopted by Strand Century.

Light pen A light pen was used for channel access in 'Autocue', an American memory lighting control of the mid 1970s. Individual channels were selected by touching the channel's displayed number on a video screen with a light pen. The system, used rather more in television studios than in theatres, did not arouse sufficient enthusiasm for it to be developed further.

L.P. Luminous preset. A board with channel grouping by a microswitch in each of the internally illuminated presetting levers.

Lightset L.P. was transformed via a simple but elegant modification into Lightset, the culmination of manual presetting – although almost immediately overtaken by the development of memory.

Strand LIGHT PALETTE

Lightwright A Rosco computer programme which organises lighting paperwork. It edits, prints and cross-references every kind of list and schedule required in the planning stages; then updates and analyses cue information during plotting and rehearsals.

Limelight The first really powerful light source capable of being deployed in a directional instrument was the limelight where the flame from a mixture of oxygen and hydrogen impinged upon a block of lime which became brilliantly incandescent.

Limes Jargon for follow spots and their operators.

Lime box Windowed room at rear of auditorium, usually behind the highest balcony, for follow spots. See also BOXED LIMES.

Linear flood A flood using a long thin double-ended halogen lamp which allows the reflector to be designed for an increased beam spread. (*Illus. p. 68.*)

Linnebach A method of shadow projection named after Adolf Linnebach who demonstrated it at Munich Opera at the beginning of the twentieth century. The source is a powerful lamp in a matt black housing, with neither reflector nor lens. The 'slide' is a large piece of artwork supported separately: moving this slide relative to lamp house and

Liquid dimmer

CCT Minuette LINEAR FLOOD

screen offers some adjustment to the sharpness and size of the image.

Liquid dimmer Liquid was often used in early resistance dimmers as an alternative to wire. Since pure water is a poor conductor, electrolytes were added, usually washing soda, salt or dilute sulphuric acid. The fluid was contained in an earthenware pot, often fabricated from a length of drainage pipe. There was a fixed electrode at the bottom and a moving one lowered from the top. These were usually cone-shaped to improve contact at the full-on position and were made of lead for acid solutions, wrought or cast iron for alkaline. The larger installations were located understage and each dimmer operated remotely by a tracker wire guided by a series of pulleys.

Load in & out See GET-IN and GET-OUT.

Load The lights controlled by an individual dimmer and limited by the rating of that dimmer. Some older dimmers were load sensitive. Although they had a tolerance either side of their rating of about one-third (a 750 watt dimmer

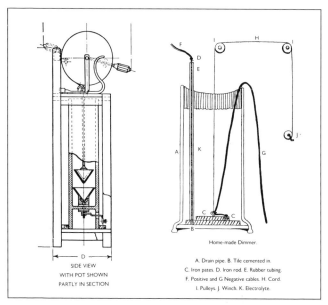

LIQUID DIMMERS (A) Professional (B) Homemade

would look happily at 500 and 1000 watts), smooth control for tightly lit dramas often required the addition of dummy loads. These were usually ancient spots and floods whose lightshow under the stage or in the flys was often rather more interesting than the performance.

Lobsterscope Older American term for a perforated wheel spun in front of a spotlight lens to give a ripple or flicker. See FLICKER WHEEL and K-K WHEEL.

Lose Take out a light (as in the request 'Lose twenty nine!').

Low voltage Most lights operate at the local supply voltage, with the world basically divided into 220/240 or 110/120. But lower voltage lamps give a more intense light than mains voltage lamps of the same wattage, and their filaments can offer some advantages for certain types of optical system. Low voltage beamlights operating at 24 volts and either 500W or 1kW are particularly attractive. The size and weight of the transformer to be incorporated in the spotlight casing is something of a drawback, although the latest toroidal transformers are somewhat lighter. The development of suitable electronic transformers could open up new low-voltage instrument possibilities.

Lumen A measure of the light output from a source. (The amount of light, from a point source of one candlepower at the centre of a sphere of one foot radius, falling upon one square foot of the surface of that sphere.)

Luminaire The international word for any lighting instrument of any kind (not just the specialised lighting instruments used in the theatre).

Lux A measure of the level of illumination on a surface. (One lumen spread over one metre.)

Magazine batten See BATTENS.

Magic sheets Originally a simplified light plan for quick reference, but increasingly a control surface (qv) providing direct channel access by touching graphics on a plan.

Magnetic amplifier A sophisticated inductance dimmer of the 1950s and 1960s with use restricted mainly to the subsidised theatres of central Europe where high cost was not a problem. It was load independent but, in the characteristic nature of chokes, slow to react. These dimmers responded to currents which were small enough to allow remote control from an all-electric solid-state preset desk. However, Siemens, the leading manufacturer of magnetic amplifiers, opted to use a motor in the desk to drive miniature faders which could be preset through polarised relays programmed by a further set of sub-miniature levers. Consequently the system was little more than a miniature version of the old direct-operated boards and shared every motorised board's inability to dim proportionally. Other manufacturers, particularly ADB and ASEA Graham, used magnetic amplifiers with proportional electrical presetting, pioneering the method that would become standard with thyristor dimmers.

Magnetic clutch Allowed a mechanical dimmer to be moved remotely. A control current from the desk energised an electro-magnet which attached the dimmer arm to the drive shaft for as long as was required to move the dimmer to its new position.

Maintained Safety lighting which is independent of the

production lighting system and is 'maintained' alight irrespective of any changes, particularly blackouts, of the stage lighting. In the event of power supply failure to the building, light continues to be 'maintained' from batteries in order to illuminate escape from the building should such an emergency evacuation become necessary.

Make-up Growth in the sculptural use of light has resulted in fundamental changes in the basic function of actor make-up. When lighting was a flat overall wash of coloured illumination, it was necessary to use make-up to emphasise the three dimensional quality of faces. This was achieved by neutralising the face with a tinted foundation and then greasepainting new facial contours with particularly exaggerated highlighting of nose and cheekbones. Sculptural light makes this not only unnecessary but look unnatural. So, when actors play their own age in a production style close to reality, normal make-up is just a light foundation with a possible slight strengthening around the eyes, including the magic touch of carmine in the corners. Heavier make-up is reserved for more non-realistic acting styles and for actors playing a different age or required to age considerably during the time span of the play. However any really extensive use of two-dimensional face painting becomes unconvincing under directional lighting and so such matters as deep scars and distorted noses require a three dimensional prosthetic treatment.

Manual controls The label 'manual controls' was originally reserved for systems where the operational lever was directly connected to the dimmer. Since the advent of computer boards, the term has been widened to include electronic systems which are preset by hand rather than by memory. Pre-electronic boards from the grandmaster to the C.D. used many ingenious devices to bring the maximum number of dimmers under the control of the minimum number of hands. The major problem of systems without presetting facilities was time. The amount of preparation that could be done between cues was limited to memorising actions required once the cue had started: once a ten second cue was underway with several channels moving to different levels, there was little possibility of studying a written plot. With little chance of introducing subtleties into the timing, operators could only aim for an overall smoothness with the delicate half-points being tweaked into place after completion of the main cue time. Electronic boards with manual presetting offer subtle timing: their limitation is the time required between cues for presetting ahead.

Maroons Pyrotechnics, fired electrically, which provide the sound effect of exploding bombs.

Masking Neutral material or scenery which defines the performance area and conceals the technical areas.

Master A lever or push which overrides (or 'masters') a complete preset, or group within a preset or a selected memory. Masters are the control surfaces which operators activate to make complex lighting changes happen and, at their best, are simple devices which allow full concentration on timing.

Master Electrician American for CHIEF ELECTRICIAN.

McCandless In *A Method of Lighting the Stage*, published in New York in 1932, Stanley McCandless provided the first logical process for lighting the stage. While the method may have been refined in a number of ways over the years, particularly by the addition of backlight, McCandless principles are still fundamental to the way in which most productions are lit today.

Memory controls Lighting control systems where channel intensities for each cue are filed automatically in an electronic store. Initially developed in the late 1960s, memory storage is now standard practice and has released operators from beat-the-clock feats of dexterity and drudgery.

MIDI Acronym for Musical Instrument Digital Interface which is a communication protocol (qv) allowing several instruments to be interconnected and played from a central keyboard or by a central timing computer. MIDI can be used to integrate the timing of memorised light changes with music.

MINI 2 Electronic shrinkage brought a rash of product names based on 'mini' and 'micro'. The Mini 2, combining compact twin-preset desks with multiple 6-way dimmer packs, opened new horizons in both low cost and portability. (The Micro 8, on the other hand, was born of a somewhat misguided wish to miniaturise the Junior 8, using thyristor dimmers.)

Microprocessors Tiny integrated circuits used to process information in computer technology. Although level memory is still the most fundamental breakthrough of the newer control technologies, dimmer levels are just one of the many types of information handled by a lighting board's microprocessors which are programmed not only to carry out the system's functions but to monitor its performance.

MIRROR BALL with rotating motor.

Mirror ball Ball, usually 12 or 16 inches in diameter, covered in small mirror segments and suspended from a motor. When rotated and spotlit from below, moving points of sparkling light are reflected everywhere. Sometimes also used to reflect lasers with stunning effect.

Mirror spots An earlier term for profile spots, particularly those using simple mirrors rather than ellipsoidal reflectors. (Until the early 1960s, no suitable 222/240 volt lamps were available for use with deep ellipsoidal reflectors.)

Mist The use of dry-ice, smoke-guns, gauzes or moving effects, to produce mist has developed considerably in recent years. Once an occasional device used in conjunction with light to produce a romantic softening, it has become a major way of enabling light to register in performance environments such as rock concerts where there is little pictorial or stuctural scenery.

Mimics On manually operated lighting boards, the operator's eye could 'read' the state of the lighting by looking at the position of the dimmer levers, but this became impossible when intensity levels were determined by sophisticated electronic memories. Early mimics were simple panels with numerals which illuminated to indicate live or selected channels, but no system today is without a dynamic display on a video monitor showing the detailed progression of every channel. In the repertoire houses of central Europe with their fixed lighting rigs on bridges, towers and galleries, there is a logic in laying-out a mimic geographically. But for theatres with flexible plugging, a simple numerical progression is more appropriate.

MMS The Modular Memory System of the mid 1970s enabled many professional theatres to equate their aspirations with their budgets. Each desk was assembled from a selection of modules to customise a system in size and facilities. Strand's marketing included printing panel options as playing cards so that desks could be planned by shuffling. The wide range of possible permutations, combined with individuality of the operators and the zeal of the consultants, ensured that there were few cries of snap!

Modelbox A computer aided design system which stores stage plans and auditorium sightlines for most British theatres. The Modelbox software programme runs on AutoCAD and enables a scene model to be viewed from various angles so that, in addition to checking sightlines for a particular auditorium, it is possible to discover the scope offered by various lighting positions. Modelbox AutoLIGHT software allows the lighting design process to be transferred from the drawing board to the computer screen, speeding up both routine drawing tasks and the assessment of the consequences of critical design decisions.

Modelling The use of light to emphasise the three dimensional sculptural quality of an object or actor's body.

Mogul screw base See GES CAP.

Moonlight The light from the moon tends to produce an all pervading monochromatic gloom. But stage tradition, reinforced by the lyrics of popular songs across the ages, prefers it to be blue and strongly directional with contrasting shafts of light and shade. The position of the moon is

MODELBOX autolight video screen displaying, in plan and section, the consequences of hanging a particular spotlight in a particular position.

mostly indicated only by the direction of its light but occasionally the actual moon appears pictorially on the stage. This may be achieved by paint or projection techniques, including replacing the shape of the moon on a backcloth with linen for translucent backlighting.

Moon box The trajectory of the moon may be simulated with a moon box – a cut-out moon backed by a light source enclosed in a box – which is moved very, very, slowly upwards and sideways by flying on a tab-track.

Motivation The major lighting statement in a scene normally needs to be motivated by a visual logic. But this does not necessarily need to be a reason that can be expressed in words. Although the logic may well be that of the natural behaviour of sun or moon, it might be determined with equal validity by the way that the form of the set suggests a natural direction of light flow.

Mouse This familiar tool of computer graphics is a possible control surface for lighting boards. Pioneered by ADB, it allows operators to make the kind of painterly strokes that have more appeal to many lighting artists than button pushing.

Moving effects Images of moving phenomena such as snow, clouds, rain, water, etc may be produced by projec-

White Light variable speed MOVING EFFECTS disk with objective lens.

tion spotlights with motor-driven discs. See individual entries for specific effects.

MSR (Medium Source Rare Earth) High efficiency discharge lamps which not only have a high colour temperature (5600°K) but produce a light which has full continuity across the entire spectrum.

Multicore cables allow lighting bars to be fed more neatly and efficiently than with a single cable for each instrument. Low-voltage multicores have traditionally provided the standard interconnection between desk and dimmers, with each channel requiring its own control line. However, digital processing now allows a system's entire data to be multiplexed for transmission down a single core to the dimmer room.

Multigroup presetting These boards combined the channel memory pistons of electro-magnetic light organs with the electronic level presetting of thyristor dimmers. The absence of inertia reduced their flexibility and the prototypes were overtaken by the arrival of level memory.

Multiplexing Passing control instructions, particularly to dimmers or remotely focusable lights, by sending all information in ultra-rapid sequence along a single circuit (usually a pair of screened wires) rather than a circuit for each control channel or function. Multiplexed signals to dimmers have to be decoded at the dimmer racks and routed to each dimmer. This is called demultiplexing (often shortened to demux).

Multi-Q A good name, used on an early American memory system, to convey the end of technological limitation to the number of cues possible in a production.

Musicals The theatre form which places the most complex demands on lighting design and technology, virtually requiring three complete rigs to cater for the differing angles and colours used for drama, dance and song.

Naturalism All light in the real world is sourced naturally by sun, moon and stars, or artificially by lamps. The extent to which stage lighting should reflect the logic of these sources depends on the style of each individual production. It is perhaps inevitable that part of the search for a production style will involve consideration of how far the acting and visual styles should depart from naturalism. Acting always tends to have its roots in at least a heightened naturalism since most plays are about people and personal relationships in a world with which the audience are familiar through life or literature. Modern settings, however, tend to offer an environment based on representational objects used in a metaphorical way which is far removed from reality. Consequently the lighting can find itself helping to form a stylistic bridge between the barely heightened realism of the acting and the virtual non-realism of a symbolic setting. However the degree of success with which lighting addresses the naturalism question will depend not so much on the extent to which it attempts to mirror nature's logic but the consistency with which it follows its chosen path.

Neon One of the earliest forms of discharge lamp was the light generated in a narrow tube filled with neon gas. It may be coloured by the use of mercury vapour and fluorescent coatings. The linear nature of the light, and the possibility of bending the tubes, led to the development of neon signs and these have been used on stage with considerable effect.

Neutral density filters Filters which reduce the intensity of the light without changing its colour.

Non-dims Channels which, for one reason or another (usually because they are controlling a type of light source or motor that is not compatible with dimmers), are only switched. They are usually independent of the board's mastering system, although located within the main control desk. See also INDEPENDENTS.

Number one spot bar The most downstage lighting bar, ideally positioned as close to the proscenium as possible.

Obedient lights See INTELLIGENT LIGHTS.

Objective The lens which focuses the sharpness of the image from a slide in a projector. Such objective lenses are a component of an optical system where a condenser lens collects light from the lamp source to provide even illumination over the slide.

OISTAT (Organisation Internationale des Scénographes, Techniciens et Architectes de Théâtre). International forum for theatre architects, designers and technicians. Most national associations are affiliated and act as hosts, in rotation, for Oistat's specialist commissions. The PQ (Prague Quadriennial) exhibitions have been a major force in stimulating the development of scenography.

Olivette American term for a simple box flood without a formal reflector but with the inside painted white or silver.

O.P. 'Opposite prompt' side of the stage – stage right, ie actor's right when facing the audience.

Open air The particular magic of light in an open air performance is the 'reverse fade' at sunset: lighting which is barely noticeable in daylight gradually taking over as dusk falls. It is smoother and subtler than any dimmer! There are, however, a number of technical problems. Most open air stages lack means of suspension and, while this can be overcome with modern trussing systems, these tend to spoil the very environmental conditions that motivate an outdoor performance. Where possible, it is surely better to light from discreet towers which are out of the direct vision of most of the audience, even if the lighting angles are less than ideal. But there are compensations: advantage can be taken of the possibility of placing backlighting on the ground from where, in the absence of borders, light can travel upwards and onwards until lost in the sky. However, there is virtually no spotlighting equipment available with the capability of withstanding the rigours of an unpredictable climate.

Opera Almost all opera is on a very large scale. Palaces and battlefields are more common than kitchens and drawing rooms. Shakespeare's Macbeth has three witches but Verdi's operatic version needs at least four dozen to sing and a further dozen to dance. The orchestra pit nearly always outnumbers the stage. Performances are given in a complex repertoire programme which, with rehearsals, may involve two complete changeovers each day. To facilitate this, opera houses have traditionally mounted their stage lighting on bridge and tower structures for access and are now installing remotely focused instruments. In smaller opera theatres, re-focusing is often accomplished with the help of tapes (qv).

Operators without whom no lighting board has anything to offer a live performance. If I may get personal for the only time in this ABC: I would like to confirm that, as a lighting designer, I am not really interested in boards – only in their operators. Given a sensitive and committed operator, the most unpromising boards will perform anything I ask. Even boards with a penchant for amnesia seem to enjoy better health under sympathetic operation.

Organ A Compton organ console became the first board to be a playable instrument rather than a technology based electricity distribution system.

Overhang Mounting a spotlight by standing it up from the bar rather than hanging it below.

Pageant A 1kW beamlight with parabolic reflector and spillrings, introduced in the early 1930s. The earliest version had a silvered glass reflector and its intense parallel beam offered a new dynamic to stage lighting. The name is derived from the first use in outdoor pageant performances. Strand withdrew pageants in the 1960s amid howls of protest from a large proportion of their customers.

The original Strand PAGEANT.

Pairing Feeding two or more lights from the same dimmer. This may be on the bar by using a splitter (twofer), either in moulded form (grelco) or made up from two sockets with short cables wired into the same plug. Alternatively, pairing may be at the socket outlet box where it has become standard British practice to provide each circuit with a pair of sockets. Pairing is also known in America as twoferring.

Palette The range of individual light beams prepared for 'painting' the stage picture. See also LIGHT PALETTE.

PALS (Precision Automated Lighting System) Strand Lighting system which enables most of their standard instruments of 1.2kW and above to be fitted with remotely operated pan, tilt & focus. See also REMOTE CONTROL (LIGHTS).

Pan Horizontal (left/right) movement of an instrument.

Pani Austrian lighting instrument manufacturing firm founded by Ludwig Pani in Vienna. Particularly renowned for high quality scenic projectors with sophisticated mechanical dimming shutters.

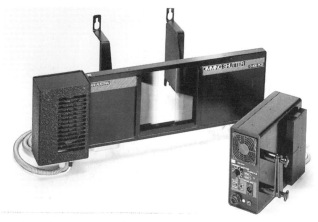

PANI Grey Scale Dimming Shutter for intensity control of HMI scene projectors: motor driven filters dim the light by progressing from clear via increasing greyness to black.

Panic switch A switch, usually at the rear of the auditorium, which overrides the houselight dimmers to enable immediate full light to be obtained in the event of an emergency.

Parcans Simple instruments which use a par lamp and therefore do not require any optical system of lenses or reflectors.

Par lamp A sealed beam lamp with the filament contained within the same glass envelope as an optical system producing a near parallel beam, elongated slightly along one axis.

Parabolic reflector Whereas spherical and ellipsoidal reflectors project a cone of light, a reflector in the form of a parabola produces a parallel beam. The beam from a true parabola will maintain a constant width whatever its length, although the cheaper reflectors inevitable in theatre luminaires tend to produce a slight widening. In sealed beam PAR lamps, with a short linear filament, the beam is assymetrical with some extension along one axis. See also BEAMLIGHTS.

Park A feature of the more sophisticated pre-memory controls which enabled channels or groups of live channels which were not actively involved in imminent cues to be transferred to a passive master where they were held, or 'parked', until once again selected to move on a cue.

Patching Patching of loads to dimmers, by a system not unlike a manual telephone exchange, was traditionally used more extensively in America than in Europe. Perhaps it was because the Americans tended to use a smaller number of higher quality dimmers while Britain opted for a large number of cheap ones. (Only subsidised central Europe could

PATCHING loads to dimmers through a patch panel.

afford a large number of quality dimmers). Also the size of 110 volt cables encourages short runs. Certainly a patching frame enabled channels to be lined up for more logical working in an era of hand operation. And it was a useful means of transferring circuits from one part of the theatre to another. But load patching is now fading into history, superseded by a soft patching programme on the control side of the dimmer. See also SOFT PATCH.

Pattern (1) Sometimes used, especially in America, for gobo. (2) Until the early 1970s all Strand lighting instruments were designated by pattern numbers. The numbers were not allocated in a logical sequence until the final years of the system when the prefix 7 in a 3-digit number indicated that the instrument was designed to use the then new 1kW tungsten halogen lamp with a GX 9.5 base.

Strand PATTERN 23 baby profile spot (lit by another pattern 23).

Pattern 23 The great classic. Britain's first small profile and the first spotlight to be tooled for manufacture from castings. In production by Strand for over thirty years from 1951 and still in regular use because of its compact shape and short length.

Pebble convex See PRISM CONVEX

Pepper's ghost An effect, popular during the nineteenth century, named after Professor John Henry Pepper who presented it at the Royal Polytechnic Institution. The ghostly image of an actor, concealed in the orchestra pit, was projected on to an invisible sheet of glass within the proscenium.

PEPPER'S GHOST

Perches Lighting positions (often on platforms) at each side of the stage, immediately behind the proscenium.

PC See PLANO CONVEX and PRISM CONVEX.

Phasing Because of the large voltages between phases in a three-phase electrical distribution system, British safety practice requires a minimum distance of six feet to be maintained between equipment on the same phase. This usually results in separate phases being allocated to the sockets foh, overstage and at stage level. Some countries, particularly those with lower voltages, do not have this requirement and it is often their established practice to wire phases consecutively in an effort to balance the load.

Photometer Instrument for measuring light quantity. Usually, but not necessarily, calibrated in lumens or lux.

Piano boards had none of the playability of organs but were the portable resistance boards which, mainly thanks to the continuing distribution of direct current and the persistence of four-wall rentals, survived on Broadway until overtaken by memory controls.

Portable resistance 'PIANO' BOARD

Pilbrow Richard Pilbrow (b.1933), British lighting design pioneer, founded Theatre Projects which gave informal training and career opportunities to many of the young designers who subsequently exercised a major influence on the development of theatre lighting. From the mid 1960s Theatre Projects became increasingly involved, as theatre consultants, in the planning of all aspects of new and refurbished theatres throughout the world.

Pile (or pile on) Adding a live preset to another which is already alive. If a channel is above zero in both presets, the highest level usually takes precedence.

Pilots Low intensity lights, often tinted blue, around the sides of the stage which do not illuminate the acting area but allow actors and crew to move about safely. Called **running lights** in America. See also WORKING LIGHTS.

Pin matrix A matrix of socket holes which, by the inser-

A PIN MATRIX as used for patching channels to back-up masters in Strand MMS control systems.

tion of small pins, allows inputs on one coordinate to be connected to outputs on another.

Pin patch (1) A pin matrix used, at the control desk, to form channels into groups where one coordinate represents channels and the other represents group masters. (2) A pin matrix used, at the control desk, to assign dimmers to channels where one coordinate represents channels and the other represents dimmers. However, both these functions are increasingly incorporated in the control desk's micro-processing software.

Pin spot A spotlight focused to light an area of very small diameter by using an instrument with a very narrow beam angle, possibly in conjunction with an iris.

Pipe American terminology for BAR.

Pipe ends Spotlights at the ends of lighting bars, crosslighting to model dancers' bodies.

Pistons allowed groups of channels, but not their levels, to be memorised. See LIGHT CONSOLE and C.D.

Plan The word 'plan' when used by lighting people without a descriptive adjective tends to refer to lighting layout plans which give information about which instruments are to be used, where they are to be hung, their colour filters, any accessories such as gobos, and their control channel numbers. This plan should contain sufficient information for an electrics crew, in the absence of the lighting designer, to rig the show and complete all preparation prior to focusing.

Plano convex lens A lens with one flat surface and one curved surface. This 'PC' lens and the fresnel lens are the alternatives normally used in stage lighting equipment.

Plasticity One of the words, similar to 'sculptural', used to describe light's capability to enhance the three-dimensional quality of an object.

Plate American. Originally a single resistance dimmer, particularly one with a curved rather than linear travel, but use extended to other forms of mechanical dimmer.

Playback The part of a desk where memorised lighting states are recalled to control the light on stage via master levers or pushes.

Plays While plays may be lit in any style, most dramas and almost all comedies require the actors' character projection to be supported by an illumination which will enable them to make eye contact with the audience. There can be some conflict in providing ideal facial visibility while maintaining a light which is sculptural, selective and appropriately atmospheric. Consequently, achieving the optimum balance is at the heart of the lighting design process.

Plots Written plots, made by each backstage department, list all the preparations and actions required during a performance. All boards need a plot, but with memory facilities the plots use less paper and the plotting takes less time.

Poached egg An old filter technique used mainly in the days when most lighting rigs consisted of a small number of primitive focus spots. A pale tint was framed by a more strongly saturated colour with a large hole cut in the centre. This gave a general ambient colour to the scene with a lighter facial tone for the acting area.

Polarised relays Utilising the wheatstone bridge principle, these allowed motor-driven dimmers to be declutched automatically on reaching a preset level.

Pole One of the earliest dimmers was a pole on which candles were mounted behind each set of wings. By rotating the pole, light could be diverted away from the stage. At DROTTNINGHOLM all the candle poles still work simultaneously from a master capstan in the prompt corner.

Pole operation Instruments arranged so that their pan, tilt and focus adjustments can be altered from floor level by a long pole rather than by climbing a ladder.

Portable It is only recently that portable has come to mean what it says: the old portable dimmers were chunky trucks of 6 or 12 resistance dimmers and required multiple heave-ho to make them even transportable. (*Illus. p. 90.*)

Portal Framed masking border bolted to framed masking legs, often given decorative treatment.

Post-office relays Prior to the development of semi-conductor switching and digital data processing, remote lighting control systems were largely dependent upon electro-magnetic relays. In Britain the standard Post Office telecom relay provided a cheap, reliable and robust component.

Practicals Light fittings which are not merely decorative but wired to light up. Also used for any prop which works.

Prefocus cap A special lamp cap which ensures that the filament lines up precisely with the optics of a spotlight.

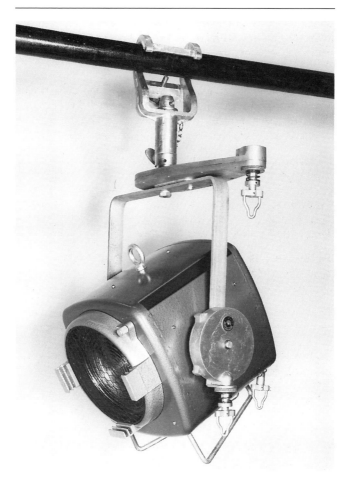

Strand Pattern 223 fresnel spotlight arranged for POLE OPERATION of pan, tilt and focus by hooking an extended lightweight alloy pole into the three rings consecutively.

Preheat When lamps are faded in from zero, there tends to be a momentary delay followed by a surge of light resulting from the warming up of a cold filament. The operator can compensate for this by momentarily pausing at the appropriate point. In some advanced systems this subtle change in tempo can be memorised as part of the fade profile. However an alternative solution, perhaps one more simple in its operation and elegant in its engineering, is for the software programme to compare the current lighting state with the next selected, identify channels at zero and supply them with just enough current to warm the filaments without producing perceivable light.

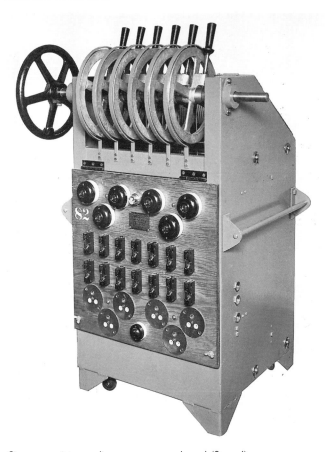

Six-way resistance dimmer PORTABLE board (Strand).

Presetting Anything which is positioned in advance of its being required – such as props placed on the stage before the performance – is said to be 'preset'. 'The preset' is the light which dresses the stage scene as the audience enter or is revealed by the rising curtain. The term is also used to describe control systems where each channel has more than one lever to allow intensity levels to be set (ie *preset*) in advance of a cue. Whether manual or memory, presetting allows preparation of a cue and reduces the number of operational hands required.

Primary colours The primary colours of light are red, blue and green. When their light beams are superimposed, they add together to produce white light. When their filters are superimposed in a single beam, they subtract all the spectrum to pass no light.

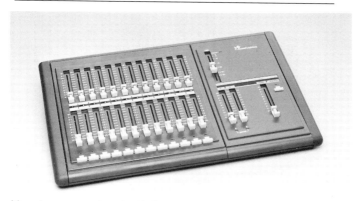

Manual PRESETTING board with 2 presets for 12 channels (Strand LX).

Prism convex lens A PC (plano convex) lens incorporating some diffusion in its structure. Also known as PEBBLE CONVEX.

Profile spots Spotlights which project the outline (ie the *profile*) of any chosen shape and with any desired degree of hardness/softness. In America usually often called ELLIPSOIDAL or LEKO.

Profiled cue A lighting change where the rates of increasing and decreasing intensities accelerate or decelerate during the progress of the change.

Projection Photographic or painted images on slides may be projected on to screens or virtually any scenic surface. Projectors use a condenser lens system to ensure an even

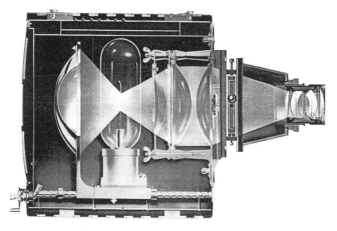

Optical system of a PROJECTION instrument with condenser and objective lenses.

light distribution over the slide, and the optical system includes heat resistant glasses to protect slides and lenses from the intense heat generated by the high intensity sources required to produce an image that will still make a positive statement when contrasted with the level of light necessary for the actors. Modern scene projectors use discharge lamps, usually HMI, and remotely controlled mechanical dimming (see PANI). Banks of 35mm Carousels controlled by computer programmes are also used.

Projection screens Choice of material to receive projection images depends primarily on whether the images will be projected from the front, from the rear or from both. Rear projection requires translucent screens which transmit an image while disguising its source. Black material is less obviously a screen when no image is present and its plastic sheen may be disguised by hanging a gauze in front. Although special screen material is likely to be necessary when clearly defined images are required, many alternative scenic surfaces offer possibilities which are appropriate to certain visual styles, particularly with the higher intensities of the new discharge sources.

P.S. 'Prompt side' of the stage – stage left, ie actor's left when facing the audience.

Proportional dimming With solid-state all-electrical systems, the progress of lights moving to their preset levels is proportional, ie all dimmers finish at the same time irrespective of the distance of travel. With mechanically driven dimmers the move was non-proportional, ie since all the dimmers travelled at the same speed, those with the shortest travel distance arrived earliest. Proportional dimming produces a more smoothly balanced cue: however in an ideal board each dimmer should be able to be given its own individual rate for each move – and in the most sophisticated systems this is possible.

Proscenium The division between audience and stage in traditional theatre forms where the audience sit in a single block facing the stage. The proscenium marking this division may take many formats from a definite picture frame arch to an unstressed termination of auditorium walls and ceiling.

Protocol The digital data processing 'language' used to transmit control information. Many manufacturers have adopted DMX512, the standard recommended by the United States Institute for Theatre Technology. This is adequate for most communications between desk and dimmers but, being a unidirectional system, is less suitable for the fault reporting capability of the newer digital dimmers and for communication with remotely operated spotlights. SMX is a newer protocol which attempts to overcome some of these limitations.

Psychedelic effects Particularly popular during the late sixties and early seventies, these were mostly produced by projecting slides made by sandwiching pigments and fluids between two pieces of glass. The heat from the projector caused the liquids to move, forming and reforming random images.

Punch cards The earliest memory boards used hole-punched cards to record cue states. Inserting new cues was a simple matter of shuffling the cards but, each time that one channel was altered half a point in rehearsal, the entire card had to be re-punched – and the printer was very noisy!

Pyrotechnics Bombs, bangs, flashes, etc.

Q is how we normally write Cue.

Q-File Thorn's Q-File had one of the most evocative names ever given to a board. Memory access and channel access were digital by columns of illuminated pushes for hundreds, tens and units, but level selection was analogue by a single lever. Since Q-File was developed prior to the rediscovery of the wheel (qv), this lever had a servo-motor which drove a selected channel rapidly and accurately to its current recorded level from where it could be modified. Although Q-File became popular in theatres, it was specifically developed for television where it was so successful that the BBC engineered a replacement in 1990 using the latest technology to implement Q-File's operational philosophy. (*Illus. p. 94.*)

Q-master had an analogue lever per channel, and prior to modification, a channel's lever had to be set at its current recorded level, with the aid of a column of pilot lights, before flicking a switch to get manual control.

Quartz lamps Alternative name for tungsten halogen lamps, arising from their envelope being made from quartz

Prototype Thorn Q-FILE with mimic panels to display the state of 200 channels and 100 memories.

rather than ordinary glass. A label more common in the early days of these lamps when, because iodine was the first halogen gas used, they were also called 'Quartz-Iodine'.

Racks For ease in connecting input power supplies, output load lines and control signals, it is customary to mount individual dimmers in racks. These racks are normally located in a central dimmer room, although individual racks may be positioned adjacent to sections (such as foh bridges, flys, etc) of a large installation. Standard racks are in multiples of 10 or 12. For small and portable situations, compact 'dimmerpacks' of 6 are common and specially flight-cased racks are available for touring. See also INTEGRAL DIMMERS.

Rail Rail, or Balcony Rail, lights are foh spotlights mounted on the fascia of an auditorium balcony. (Mostly an American term.)

Rainbows Since rainbows are formed by the prismatic break-up of 'white' light into a banded gradation of its constituent colours, it is possible to produce stage rainbows in this way. The alternative to a light source and prism is projection of a slide of a painted rainbow. This usually provides more control, not just of size and shape but of quality – like many things in the theatre, rainbows tend to have more credibility if their 'reality' is exaggerated. So slide projection is the normal method.

Rating The maximum and minimum power in kilowats that can be controlled by a circuit or dimmer.

Reactor dimmers See CHOKE DIMMERS, L.C., MAGNETIC AMPLIFIERS.

Realism Perhaps reality can never quite be achieved on a stage – communication to any but the very smallest audience requires at least a minimal strengthening of speech and movement, resulting in what is often called 'heightened reality'. The extent to which stage lighting is 'real' involves a style decision about the extent to which the light will endeavour to behave as it would in a real life environment. See NATURALISM.

Rear projection Images projected from a projector situated behind a screen. (Note: 'Back Projection' is generally held to mean images at the back of the stage, projected from either the front or rear of the screen.) Rear projection with conventional scene projectors requires considerable stage depth behind the screen, although a bank of carousels can be very much closer. Special screen materials are available for rear projection.

Recall Selecting a lighting state from a control system's memory, prior to replaying it as a replacement for the state currently on the stage.

Receptacle An American alternative for 'socket'.

Record Plotting a cue state by filing it in the electronic data storage of a memory board.

Reflection Every object reflects light to at least a minimal degree and this enables the eye to see it. Light striking a matt surface will be subject to *diffuse reflection*, with the irregular surface returning incident light at a multitude of angles so that the surface appears uniformly bright. With a polished surface all light is returned in a single and opposite direction with the angle of reflection equalling the angle of incidence. This *specular reflection* results in a controlled emergent light along a directional path. Theatre spotlights use either spherical or ellipsoidal reflectors to collect maximum light from their lamp sources. See also PARABOLIC REFLECTOR.

Reflector cloth Translucent backcloths, particularly those made from plastic materials, are best lit from behind by bouncing light off a reflector cloth of plain white canvas (it may even be an old painted cloth hung back to front). The resultant light on the backcloth is not only softly diffused but having the light upstage of the backcloth ensures that ambient light does not spread downstage. This allows actors or objects to be shown in a clean silhouette, if desired. Reflector cloths are called **bounce cloths** in America.

Refraction The bending of light rays when passing from one transparent material to another. A lens controls light by differential refraction of all the constituent rays falling upon it so that they all converge at a focal point.

Rehearsals Production lighting is normally used only at technical rehearsals and dress rehearsals.

Relays were the backbone of remote control in pre-electronic days. Banks of basic telecom type relays selected channels and polarised relays transmitted levels. The climax of relay technology was probably the Compton Organ system which could capture groups of channels for memorised recall.

Remote control (boards) Whereas directly operated boards have a necessarily short mechanical connection between dimmers and operational levers, remote control boards have an electrical connection which can be reasonably long and indirect. This allows the dimmers to be sited in the optimum position for circuit distribution, while the desk is placed to give the operator both a good view and a good contact with the stage. Earlier remote boards used electro-magnetic control of a motor-driven mechanical dimmer bank but, with the advent of the thyristor dimmer, all remote connections became electrical and now often use multiplexed digital protocols.

Remote control (lights) Remote control of lights goes back to pre-electricity days of gas, oil and candle when the technology was based on lines guided by pulleys. Devices such as rods and bicycle brake linkages all have an honourable history but motors have been used increasingly over the last forty years. Initially, control was by sets of up, down and stop buttons for pan, tilt and focus. Then polarised relays were added to enable presetting on dials calibrated in degrees. Early memorising used cassette tapes, but control is now fully computerised and can be integrated with intensity control in the main lighting desk with digital instructions for all functions transmitted along a single circuit. However,

Strand Cantata profile spot fitted with PALS REMOTE CONTROL of pan and tilt.

perhaps the major recent advance has been in repeat accuracy which is very critical because very small movement errors at the instrument may be magnified in transmission over the distance to the stage to an extent that the light misses the actor.

Rental Most equipment used on tour or in London's West End and New York's Broadway is rented rather than owned by the production companies. Apart from simplifying the accountancy of productions which are capitalised as individual investment opportunities, renting allows the use of the most appropriate equipment, maintained to the highest standards.

Repertoire A form of organisation where two or more productions alternate in the course of a week's performance programme.

Resistance dimmers An older mechanical form of dimmer which reduces the flow of electrical current to a light by progressively increasing the resistance to it. Much of the surplus is converted into heat.

Response Although today's thyristor dimmers have a fast and consistent response, it was not always thus: earlier dimmers had varying response times with chokes being particularly slow. Indeed the difference was such that it was not unusual for touring stage managers to have to vary cue positions according to the type of dimmer in a particular theatre. With today's dimmers, the only variables are the personal response times of the stage manager and board operator.

Retrofit Adapting an older piece of equipment to use more modern technology, eg newer lamps or better shutter assemblies.

Rheostat Old name for a resistance dimmer.

Rigger's control A portable hand-held control unit which allows channels or groups to be switched remotely from the stage for focusing when the control room is unmanned. Rigger's controls may transmit their information by wire or wireless.

Rigging The positioning of lighting equipment on bars, trusses, booms, ladders, etc, as appropriate; fitting colour frames and accessories such as barndoors and gobos; cabling it to the socket outlets from the dimmers; and flashing out to ensure that every instrument is working and fed from the correct channel ready for focusing.

Rim light Backlighting which creates a 'rim' of light around the actors to separate them from their background.

Road board American term for a touring company's control board.

Rock Lighting rig and loudspeaker stacks are the major element in the scenic environment of most rock concerts. Therefore the visual effect of the lights can be just as important as the light they give. Massed parcans meet both requirements: their light output allows the use of saturated colour filters, and these filters give positive images, particularly when flashing and chasing. In the absence of scenery, smoke provides a surface upon which the light may register.

Rockboards Control boards with particularly flexible facilities for 'playing' channels or groups and for setting up complex sequences for flashing and chasing.

Rosco Roscolab are perhaps the most adventurous colour filter manufacturers and are at the forefront of the development of diffusers.

Roscolux See SUPERGEL.

Bytecraft RIGGER'S CONTROL enables the remote switching of channels and memories when no operator is present in the control room.

Celco Gold control desk with facilities appropriate for designer operation of all forms of performance, including ROCK, where instant channel access is a priority.

Rosenthal Jean Rosenthal (1912–69) was the major pioneer of lighting design in the United States – particularly as an art form.

Rotary masters Most of the remote control desks associated with thyratron and choke dimmers, and many of the earlier thyristor desks, used rotary rather than linear masters for their presets. Although this was done for electrical reasons (the heavier control currents required by most earlier dimmers), many operators favoured them for smooth operation of slow cues.

Rondel A round, convex heat resistant glass filter still to be found in some American borderlights (battens) and footlights.

Running lights See PILOTS.

Safeties American term for the various safety devices (chains, cables, ropes, etc) used to secure instruments, booms, tools, etc to ensure that they will not fall.

Safety There are two major risk areas for lighting safety on a stage. The first is diminished concentration arising from tiredness. The other is cutting corners in a spirit of 'The show must go on'. Mechanical accidents are more common than electrical ones. Provided that equipment is well maintained and basic commonsense procedures followed in its use, electrical accidents are unlikely. But spanners left at the top of ladders are lethal. Spotlights with loosely tightened hook clamps may be knocked off bars but they will not fall provided they have safety chains. Continual vigilance is the only safeguard.

Samoiloff In the 1920s, Adrian Samoiloff created a considerable stir by exploiting complementary colours to create magic effects. A pure red object under light which has been filtered to primary red will be interpreted by the human eye as reddish white; under cyan (blue-green) light it will appear black. So Samoiloff dressed an actor with red make-up in a coat of black and blue-green stripes: under red light this actor appeared as a white man in a black coat while blue-green light changed him to a black man in a striped coat.

Similar use of coloured light and paint was used to change the appearance of scenery, particularly in relation to the seasons, and the technique became known as the 'Samoiloff effect'. Historically, Samoiloff's use of filters is also interesting because its need for pure concentrated colour, coupled with its demonstration of filtered light's superiority, triggered off the changeover from lacquered lamps to compartment battens on British stages.

Saturated colours Colours with a strong hue, relatively undiluted, which absorb a considerable proportion of the spectrum.

Saturable reactors Simpler inductance dimmers using direct current saturation of the iron cores in heavy chokes. This required large currents which made presetting networks difficult to design. Response was slow and the load had to be matched to the dimmer's rating, with a ratio of 2:1 as the viable maximum.

Saturation rig A type of repertoire theatre lighting installation where maximum numbers of spotlights are rigged in every available position.

Scales for many years, the commonest dimmer scale was 0–10 and this still lingers, despite a computer board's preference for displaying percentages. Many older designers still call for 'point five' rather than 'fifty per cent'. The really old ones tend to call for a half because they date from an era when, although most dimmers had ten-point scales, it was optimistic to hope for even quarter, half and three-quarters on a very fast show. In the fastest shows it even needed some luck to get total accuracy on full and out, although on slowish plays a good operating team could deliver such finesse as a quarter plus or minus. German manual boards used a scale that seemed upside-down to most of the rest of the world: out was at the top and full at the bottom.

Scatter Low intensity light cast outside the main beam of a lighting instrument.

Scene projection See PROJECTION.

Scenography The international term for all aspects of design where the visual environment is an integral constituent of the production rather than just a decorative addition.

Schedules (1) Careful scheduling is central to efficient management of the lighting process. Technical stage time is always short, often even shorter than money, and is particularly critical for lighting since possibilities can be neither explored nor demonstrated in a rehearsal room. Acute shortage of rigging and focusing time will certainly restrict the amount of equipment that may be rigged, and possibly the degree of artistic risk that may be incorporated in the design. The essence of good scheduling is accurate assessment of the time necessary to complete each task, coupled with maximum integration of the work of each staging department. (2) Schedule is also the general word, especially in America, for tables of data, eg instrument schedule, control schedule etc.

Schwabe German manufacturing firm, prominent in the 1920s and 1930s and particularly associated with lighting equipment for cycloramas which were then at the height of their popularity as a staging style. See HORIZON FLOOD, CLOUD MACHINE and ACTING AREA (2).

Sciopticon American term for optical effects disc projectors.

Scoop A simple directional floodlight with a reflector which is also the lamp house. Used mainly in television studios as a softlight and now obsolescent.

SCR (Silicon Controlled Rectifier) The device, now more commonly known outside the United States as a THYRISTOR, which revolutionised dimming in the mid 1960s. Since they work as ultra-rapid switches, they brought a new life, even accuracy, to the word 'switchboard'.

Screens See PROJECTION SCREENS.

Screw Cap A simple lamp base, used only for battens, floods and older spotlight types. See PREFOCUS.

Scrim Alternative word for GAUZE (mainly American).

Scroller Colour changer where a roll of filters are taped together and positioned by a very fast motor. Usually activated by digital signals from a control system which often includes a memory facility.

Sculptural light Whereas frontal light tends to flatten any object or actor, light from the side enhances third dimensional depth and emphasises sculptural quality.

Sectional drawings A particularly critical aspect of lighting design is the angle at which light hits the actor or scenic object. The designer, therefore, needs access to drawings showing a section of the stage with scenery and lighting positions. The most common section, that through the centreline, shows the basic information. However it cannot be precise about the oblique angles at which most lights hit their target: virtually every light would need its own draw-

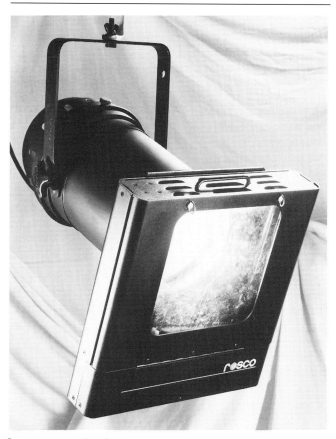

Rosco SCROLLER fitted to parcan.

ing. This being impractical, lighting designers have to rely on experience to refine the accuracy of the guesswork with which they allow for the effects of cross-lighting angles. But computer aided design is removing the need to guess: the screen can show a sectional view of the path of any beam, and the elliptical shape of the image projected on the surface upon which it lands.

Segue Musical term for one number to follow another without a break. Used in theatre to indicate immediate continuity of all kinds.

Selectivity Whereas a film or video director may make a precise selection of audience vision by framing with the camera, a theatre audience looks at all of the stage all of the time. Concentrating audience vision on a particular part of the stage is therefore a major role for theatre lighting. Selection may be such that the audience is consciously aware, or its effect may be totally subconscious, with an infinite range of subtlety in between.

Semiconductors Materials which transmits electricity better than insulators but less well than conductors. Their major importance in stage lighting control technology is in devices which allow currents to flow in one direction only.

Sequential crossfade Most controls have a 'sequence' option which automatically recalls the next memory file in numerical sequence and assigns it to the preset side of the playback crossfader. Linking facilities allow alternative memory numbers to be interpolated into the sequence. Sequential crossfading, with lighting states progressively replaced by different states, is arguably the core function of a lighting desk.

Servo A system in which information from a controlled device is fed back to help with the control of that device. Servo circuits, using polarised relays, were added to the electro-magnetic clutches of motor-driven banks so that each dimmer would de-clutch as soon as it had been driven to the level which was preset on a lever at a remotely sited desk. The servo principle is also at the heart of many remotely controlled spotlights, the polarised relays of the early models having been overtaken by computation methods which are increasingly digital.

Setting Obsolete word for the process of adjusting the beams and direction of spotlights. Use of the word 'focusing' which, strictly speaking, refers to adjustments of image clarity, has now been expanded to include the whole setting process.

Shadows One of the most difficult aspects of stage lighting design is the control of shadows. Every light casts a shadow of the object or actor that it hits. In nature, these shadows indicate clearly the direction of the light's travel from a single source – sun, moon or chandelier. On a stage, however, the need to give actors sculptural visibility over a long distance requires a multiplicity of sources. Normally the key, or motivational, direction of the light will be the strongest visual statement and can be emphasised by undertaking what amounts to a damage limitation programme to reduce the impact of shadows from non-motivational sources. This entails such ploys as careful choice of angles in an attempt to throw shadows on the floor where they will be washed out by other lights (but beware trying to wash out shadows on walls by raising brightness to a level that throws actors into silhouette). Or making edges of beams coincide with lines on the set and therefore be less noticeable. Or texturing the light so that shadows are broken up.

Shadow projection Shadow puppetry is one of the earliest forms of theatre and its techniques, basically unchanged, remain in use both as a free-standing perform-ance medium and as an effect in productions of all kinds. The puppets are manipulated behind a screen on to which images are projected from a single light source. (Multiple sources produce multiple images, one per source, and so are only used occasionally for special effect). The best source is a lamp with neither lens nor reflector but with a housing which provides some containment of the beam to the appropriate size and shape over the desired throw distance. The size of the image depends on the placing of the puppet between source and screen and this can be varied to provide a dramatic zoom. For shadow projection of static scenery see LINNEBACH.

Shift allows a set of control surfaces on a desk to perform more than one function. This is common practice in the design of today's boards. The term and the technique was used in Strand's experimental punch card board of 1959. Was this the first shift?

Shin busters Lights mounted at or near stage floor level, used mainly for dance.

Shutters Blades, usually four, placed at the GATE (optical centre) of a profile spotlight to allow the beam to be trimmed to any four-sided shape.

Side arm See BOOM ARM.

Siemens Pioneering German firm of lighting manufac-turers, noted for the quality of their engineering.

Sightlines Lines drawn on plan and section to indicate limits of audience vision from extreme seats, including side seats, front and back rows, and galleries.

Silhouette (1) An actor or object appearing as a dark two-dimensional shaped outline against a lighter background. The cleanest silhouettes are obtained against a backlit translucent cloth (see REFLECTOR CLOTH). Any light on the actor or object should be from behind and used with particular care if the stage floor has a reflective surface. (2) CCT's pioneering variable beam profile spotlight. (*Illus. p. 106.*)

Silks Diffusion filters which stretch the light in a chosen direction.

CCT SILHOUETTE variable beam profile spot

Slider dimmer The simplest resistance dimmer was the slider making a direct contact with a portion of a continuous resistance winding. Some autotransformer dimmers, particularly those made in America by Ariel Davies, had a sliding action.

Slides The standard slide (diapositive) sizes for high power scenic projectors are 18cm × 18cm and 24cm × 24cm. These are large enough to be painted by hand or may be produced photographically. However, much projection is from banks of carousel type equipment using 35mm slides which are much cheaper to photograph and easier to change rapidly, utilising the large capacity of their standard magazines.

Slots Side lighting positions incorporated within auditorium walls.

Smoke A light beam passing through the air registers its presence by reflecting off particles of dust or moisture. With clean air legislation reducing smog, and with theatres banning tobacco, the choice of whether to see or not to see a

Structure of resistance SLIDER DIMMER.

light beam has become a much more manageable situation. The standard technique is to inject small quantities of smoke into the air by vapourising special smoke fluids which are not harmful to lungs. The 'smoke guns' used for this are becoming increasingly sophisticated but considerable care is still required in their use, particularly as the different atmospheric conditions in an empty and full auditorium can make results unpredictable despite intensive rehearsal. Smoke is lighter than air: for a heavy vapour that remains at floor level see DRY ICE. (*Illus. p. 108.*)

SMX See PROTOCOL.

Snap cues Instant light changes, ie with a fade time of zero seconds. Snap applies particularly to cues which take the

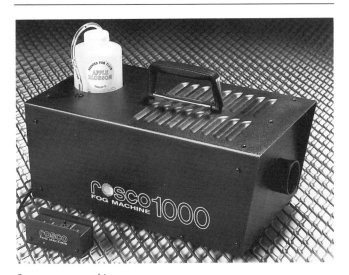

Rosco SMOKE machine

light to or from blackout. Snap cues which take the light instantly from one picture to another are usually called CUT cues.

Snoot See HAT.

Snow Falling snowflakes may be projected with an optical effects disc. Considerable care in focusing is required to avoid an impression of floating golfballs: a metal mask with lots of small perforations may be helpful in sharpening the image. For a physical representation of a snowfall, flakes of paper or polystyrene may be released above the stage and crosslit. The traditional 'snow bag' is a piece of canvas suspended from two adjacent fly bars. Movement of the bars causes the 'snow' to fall through slits in the canvas.

Soap bubbles A soap bubble machine is just one of the more occasional effects to be found in the catalogues. (Well, soap bubbles do become very prismatic under light, but what about the half-kilo of confetti that leaps on cue from a confetti cannon?)

Socapex A system of multi-pin plugs and sockets used for feeding spotbars and for connecting to touring dimmer racks.

Society of British Theatre Designers (**SBTD**) A forum for designers working in all areas of scenery, costume and lighting to share information and exchange views. The Society was formed by expansion of the Society of British Theatre Lighting Designers (ie, by removing the word 'lighting'), although lighting designers now also have their own specialist Association of Lighting Designers.

Soft light A diffuse light which produces illumination with minimum shadows.

Softlight An instrument, used mainly in television, designed to produce a soft light. The amount of diffusion incorporated to make the light as shadowless as possible results in a light too uncontrolled for a stage environment where light has to undertake many of the selective functions carried out by camera framing in a studio.

Soft patch An electronic facility within a control system to allow dimmers to be allocated to channels as required. Particularly useful for touring because it allows each light to have the same channel number in every venue.

Solenoid The movement induced in a piece of metal (known as a slug) by the magnetic field produced by passing current through a cylindrical coil of wire. This provided the mechanism for one of the earliest forms of remotely operated semaphore colour change. A group of switches allowed the required colour frames to be preset for a move which took place when the solenoids were energised by a master push.

Solid state A situation, particularly in intensity control, where all action is carried out electronically without moving parts. Nothing appears to be happening and so 'solid state' includes thyristors but excludes thyratrons which can be seen to light up although their emitted electrons are invisible.

Son et lumière An entertainment usually out-of-doors at night and often associated with telling the history of a building. An audio tape is coordinated with a series of visual effects based mainly on lighting changes.

S.P. (Standard Preset) The up-market cousin of J.P. (qv) control systems when Strand brought thryistor presetting to the mass market in the second half of the 1960s. It was available in versions with either two or three presets, and a set of grouping switches allowed each channel to be routed to alternative masters. Although there were a pair of masters for each preset, the grouping was common to all presets and this considerably reduced the operational flexibility of the system. (*Illus. p. 110.*)

Specials Most instruments in a production rig are focused for several functions, particularly those lighting small areas which combine to form larger ones. But a few are focused

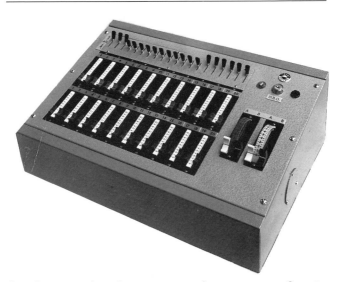

Strand twenty channel s.p. system with two presets. Grouping switches allowed each channel to be grouped to the A or B masters or to both.

for one special task – usually so special that they are usable for that moment only. Inexperienced lighting designers need to beware of falling into the trap of using too large a proportion of their resources for specials so that the production has a few short wonderful moments at the expense of the rest of a long evening.

Special effects (1) An all-embracing term covering all theatrical effects including lighting, sound, pyrotechnics, stage illusions etc. When applied to lighting it covers the use of light for reasons other than those connected with illumination. (2) A switch-fuse power supply for connection of a touring company's boards. (**Company switch** in America.)

Specular reflection See REFLECTION.

Spigot An adapter screwed to the hanging bolt of an instrument to enable it to be mounted on a floor stand.

Spill Stray or scatter light outside the main beam.

Split colour See COMPOSITE GELS.

Split fader Really means 'split crossfader'. Two masters mounted side-by-side, with one upside down, so that when moved together by one hand the incoming preset or memory will take over while the outgoing fades.
Alternatively they may be moved with two hands at differ-

ent speeds so that the incoming light leads or lags the outgoing.

Splitter Two sockets on short cables wired into the same plug, or a moulded adapter (grelco), used for feeding two lights from one cable. Also known as **Twofer**.

Spot(light) (1) An instrument providing control of the angle of the emerging light beam and therefore of the size of area lit. (2) To narrow the beam of a spotlight so that it covers a smaller area.

Spot line A temporary line dropped from the grid to suspend something in an exact special position.

Spread The area of light covered by a light beam. As most instruments (except beamlights) produce a cone of light, the spread will increase with the throw distance between instrument and actor or object to be lit.

Square rig A suspended lighting rig using bars running up and downstage in addition to the normal bars across the stage. Looks rather like the modular grids associated with thrust stages and tends to be used in a similar way – lighting the actor from 4 angles at 90°. Since square rigs block flying lines, their use is limited to productions with few fly cues.

Stage management The stage management team are in overall control of the performance and responsible for signalling the cues that coordinate the work of the actors and technicians. In British theatre, the deputy stage manager normally calls the cues and so is crucial to the timing of lighting changes.

Stalls control Allows board operation at rehearsal from the production desk position in the auditorium. Although some light consoles had a sufficiently long control cable to make this feasible, the first board to be specifically planned for use in this way (and regularly so used) was probably the Glyndebourne installation of 1964. The design required a lot of multicore and relays for a facility that now needs but a single circuit for data transmission.

Standards Various bodies around the world set and/or monitor standards for all aspects of stage lighting, particularly the inherent safety of equipment and the adoption of safe operational procedures. The somewhat ad hoc tradition of setting local standards is moving to an increasingly formal situation, particularly within the European Community and, while everyone unreservedly respects the need for the highest possible safety standards, there is considerable concern about possible blanket imposition of regulations without proper consideration of their suitability for the specialised circumstances of the theatre industry.

Stand by The signal given shortly before a cue, to warn an operator that the cue is imminent.

Standing Scenery ('standing set') or lights ('standing light') which do not charge during the performance.

Stands Lights on stands are used much less frequently than in the days when backstage practice was more labour intensive than it is now. Traditional stands were slim, with short but heavy bases, whereas today's are lighter with wider bases, usually tripoid and often wheeled. Stands now tend to be used in productions with few scenery changes, and in situations where they can be located clear of actor traffic. Use in conjunction with scene changes requires supervision by a stage electrician.

Stars Stars may be projected with gobos or slides. However in most situations, it is more effective to use a light-emitting source. The traditional method of tiny pea lamps pushed through holes in a black backcloth has been overtaken by FIBRE OPTICS (qv).

Stencils Scale stencils, usually at 50:1 and 25:1, with outlines of all types of lighting instrument are available for drawing lighting plans. Called **Drafting Templates** in America.

Stelmar An early profile spot (1929) with spherical reflector behind the source and paired concentric ellipsoidal reflectors between source and gate. Used with tungsten lamp for foh and with carbon arc as followspot.

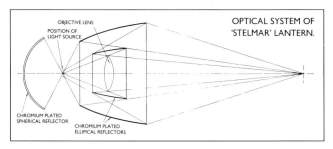

STELMAR optics.

Stopkeys The finger-tab selectors of the Compton organ were adapted by Bentham for channel access on his light console. With its stopkey depressed, a channel was selected to move when the appropriate keys were played on the keyboard. When a stopkey was pressed harder, moving it through to 'second touch', its circuit level was registered on a dial on the console desk.

Strand In 1914 two theatre electricians formed The Strand Electric & Engineering Co Ltd which was taken over in 1969 by the Rank Organisation who first called it Rank Strand Electric and now call it Strand Lighting. Once known to the theatre lighting fraternity as The Strand and now just Strand, the firm has been at the heart of the development of 'lighting for entertainment' – to quote their old advertising slogan. Many of the important advances in stage lighting were made either because Strand did it or because someone else reacted against the way Strand were doing it. Their influence was particularly strong during the great British theatre boom of the 1960s and early 1970s when there was a great surge of new playwriting and theatre building, accompanied by new horizons in direction and design. Throughout this period, Strand made their Covent Garden showrooms available for catalytic meetings of technicians, designers and architects, while their magazine *Tabs* recorded, provoked and generally stimulated. See also BENTHAM.

Stray light Uncontrolled light, including emissions through ventilation holes in equipment, spill from unshielded worklights, reflections, etc.

Strip limes Flooding follow spots to cover the whole stage, using the top and bottom shutters to produce a strip of light cut off at the front of the stage and at actor head height. To box limes is essentially the same, although perhaps used more for covering the whole proscenium opening rather than just to head high (see BOXED LIMES).

Strobe Device giving a fast series of very short light flashes under which action appears to be frozen.

Stud-contact Stud-contact dimmers had a series of individual resistances selected by a sweeping arm.

Style The contribution made by lighting to any performance is related to the acting and visual styles chosen for that particular production and agreed by the production team. There are no absolute rules about what constitutes good lighting. Most lighting styles embrace a basis of sculptural visibility but this is not absolutely necessarily so. Wider options which may or may not be present in the stylistic mix are light's capability to concentrate vision and/or support atmosphere. And a major component will be question of how far the light should attempt to accord with the logic of

Wallmounting SUNSET resistance dimmer.

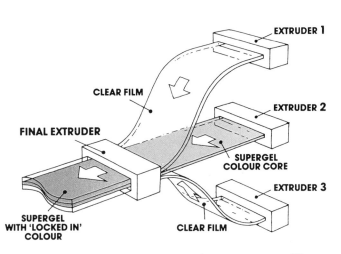

The structure, and indication of the manufacturing process, of Rosco SUPERGEL high temperature filter.

nature's sun, moon and stars – or firelight and chandeliers. Style in any area is dependent for its credibility upon consistency and lighting is no exception.

Submaster Master fader for a group of channels within a preset. The group may be permanent, or selected by switching as required.

Subtractive colour mixing See COLOUR MIXING.

Sun Audience perception of brightness is dependent upon contrast and this is particularly so in the case of sunlight. A slight tinting with pale yellow plus perhaps just the tiniest hint of palest green can help. But credibility requires not just strong directional shafts but the positive shadows which are thrown and the positive areas of shade which are created. In general, projected images of the sun are unconvincing although a painted sun on a cloth can be much more believable, probably because there is no pretence at reality.

Sun burner Situated in the centre of the auditorium ceiling, the sun burner was not only the principal houselight in the gas era but provided a ventilation system by accelerating the upward flow of spent air and its expulsion through a roof duct.

Sunset dimmers These were stud contact type, often wall-mounted for houselights or incorporated in bracket handle boards.

Sunspot Strand carbon arc follow spot which was standard in most major British theatres prior to the arrival of CSI and HMI sourced equipment. Sunspots were generally more mechanically sophisticated than the follow spots which replaced them.

Supergel Rosco colour filter (known as **Roscolux** in America) specially fabricated to withstand the effects of the new hotter lamps. The colour is not coated on a single surface but laminated between two layers of clear polycarbonate film.

Super trouper A follow spot made by Strong. See also TROUPER. (*Illus. p. 116.*)

Svoboda (1) Josef Svoboda (b. 1920), Czech scenographer who pioneered the development of light as an integral feature of visual theatre, particularly utilising projection and high intensity low voltage backlight. (2) A backlighting batten with each unit comprising nine 24v narrow beam lamps in series. (*Illus. p. 116.*)

Swatch books Sample books of colour filters. The filters

Strong SUPER TROUPER xenon follow spot

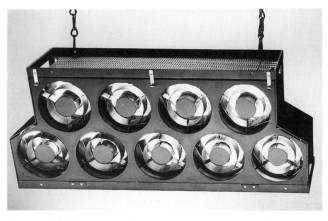

Section of ADB SVOBODA low voltage narrow beam backlight.

may be arranged either in numerical order or in colour groups. Where the manufacturer does not produce both, lighting people often rearrange a second book to have both options available. Selecting a colour while designing is easiest from a book arranged in colour sequence, whereas numerical order is more convenient when preparing filters in a workshop.

Switchboard Still used casually for all control systems however elaborate, although dimmers as well as switches have been included in lighting controls from their earliest days, including gas.

Symbols The symbols used to designate instruments on lighting plans are of two kinds. Normally a lighting designer will wish to draw precise indications of particular models and will use a stencil with scaled outlines recognisable as manufacturers' models. However there are also a series of internationally agreed symbols for each of the families of instruments (ie fresnels, profiles, etc). These simple outlines, which are easy to draw freehand, can be useful for international touring and illustrating magazine articles. See C.I.E.

Tablet switches Three-way switches, which eliminated labels by having space for engraved names and/or channel numbers, were used for forming groups on most of the Strand remote control desks of the 1950s and early 1960s. (*Illus. p. 118.*)

Tabs (1) Originally 'tableaux curtains' which drew outwards and upwards. Now generally applied to any curtain, including a vertically flying front curtain (house tabs) and, especially, a pair of horizontally moving curtains which overlap at centre and move outwards from that centre. (2) *Tabs* was the house magazine of The Strand Electrical and Engineering Company, subsequently known as Rank Strand Electric and currently as Strand Lighting. Tabs was first published in 1937 and, especially in the period from 1960 to 1977, was a major source of information not only on stage lighting but on theatre architecture.

Tab warmers (Curtain Warmers in America) Sometimes called Tab dressing. Lighting for the main house curtain. The

Three position engraved TABLET SWITCHES.

most excitingly theatrical light is probably the uplight from footlights but these have virtually disappeared as standard equipment and are only specially installed for occasional productions. Some spotlighting is therefore specially focused for the tabs when they are in use: this is often a pair of fresnels on the lowest circle front.

Tail Short length of heat resistant cable attached to a lighting instrument. Traditionally wired direct, but now increasingly via a shrouded plug incorporated within the casing.

Tallescope The standard means of access to onstage lighting bars in British Theatre, the tallescope is a vertical extending alloy ladder on a wheeled base, topped by a small enclosed working platform just big enough to hold one person. The four wheels on the base can be adjusted to different heights to compensate for a stage floor rake, or positioned across rostra of varying heights. Outriggers provide stability to compensate for the short wheel base and it is customary to have two people (three on a steep rake) pushing the tallescope and holding it steady while in use.

Tape focusing A method of quick focusing on stages playing in repertoire. New productions are lit in the normal way, focusing from ladders. After cues have been plotted and the scenery struck, the positions of the light beams on the bare floor are recorded by using a grid reference provided by unrolling two canvas strips known as 'tapes' – one running upstage and downstage on the centre line and the other across stage on the setting line. With the crossing point as zero, the tapes are marked with a numerical scale, prefixed L or R for left and right across the stage and + or − for upstage and downstage of the setting line. Combined with records of lens knob positions and notes about edge shape and quality, tapes provide surprising accuracy when the lights are re-focused – a fast process with a tallescope wheeled over a bare stage.

Teak boards took their name from the wood on which their slider resistance dimmers were mounted. A rather alarming feature in retrospect, presumably a leftover from their direct current origins, was that the switches were in the live lines and the dimmers in the neutrals. Both were fused.

Portable resistance dimmer TEAK BOARD.

Technical rehearsal A rehearsal to integrate the actors with their technical environment. Concentration at a 'tech' is on the coordination of actors and cues rather than the finer nuances of acting.

Templates (1) American alternative for GOBO. (2) Stencils of lighting instrument outlines, normally at 1:25 or 1:50 scale, used for plan drawing.

Tenth-peak angle Sometimes known as 'field angle'. The point in a light beam where the intensity falls away to one tenth of its peak value.

Texture Light may be absolutely smooth and even, or it

may be broken up to any desired extent from almost imperceptible to very obvious graduations of light and shade. Some texturing is possible by careful mixing of overlapping beams, but gobos provide much more control. A wide catalogue range of break-up gobos of alternative size, shape and configuration are available, or they may be home-made by cutting irregular holes in heat-resistant foil. The critical factor in their use is the degree of hardness/softness with which they are focused. Superimposed gobos from several instruments usually provide a more interesting texture, particularly if they are given slightly different focuses. However, as more and more textured beams are superimposed, each one generally needs slightly harder focusing. Actors and scenery moving in textured light can provide a particularly interesting chiaroscuro. Scenery will often accept higher levels of light if it is textured, and this can be very useful in such situations as operatic moonlight.

Theatre-in-the-round A form of staging where audience totally encircle the acting area.

Three-in-line A 15amp connector which was long used for connecting stage lighting equipment of British origin. With mainly 15amp BS sockets in the flys (although, well into the 1960s, many battens and some spot bars were still directly wired to terminal boxes) and special 25amp wooden-headed plugs in the dips, fit-ups required detailed cable schedules and plug-changing was a way of life.

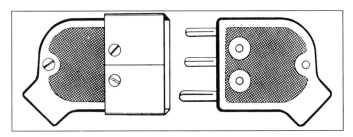

The old THREE-IN-LINE British connector.

Threeset A board providing three presets, each with three groups. These groups could be formed independently within each preset rather than be common to all presets – a victory for the user over Strand's then current Bentham philosophy.

Throw The distance between a light and the actor or object being lit.

Thrust A form of stage which projects into the auditorium so that the audience are seated on at least two sides.

Thyratron dimmers Valve dimmers which were load independent but not very stable. And this instability was of an unforgivable kind: they failed full-on rather than off.

THYRATRON DIMMER rack with three valves (one per phase) for each dimmer.

Thyristor (Also known as SCR, particularly in America – Silicon Controlled Rectifier) Electronic device which chops the wavelength of an alternating current. The thyristor dimmer is very stable (to old board operators, almost to the point of boredom) and has been the standard dimmer for over twenty years. Successors are said to be in development, but do we need them?

Tilt Vertical (up/down) movement of an instrument.

Timing Timing is perhaps the most crucial factor in any theatre performance. It is the subtleties of different timing from performance to performance that make live theatre alive. These differences are measurable in beats rather than seconds, although they can add up to several minutes on the total performance running time between such extremes as a comedy played on Wednesday matinees and Saturday nights. Timing differences may influence the moment when a lighting cue is started; they rarely effect the length of a lighting cue but they do influence the profile of the rate of change within the overall total cue time. The timing of blackouts is particularly critical in comedy: with slow responding audiences, a laugh may be dependent upon the stage manager delaying the giving of a cue by a beat. The profile of a cue – its accelerations, decelerations, leading or lagging of incoming and outgoing states, pauses etc – may be influenced by the tempo. If an actor lingers over an exit, the operator may need to hold back slightly on the progress of a cue then speed up its end. Most boards have optional memorising of cue timing and some will memorise a profile. In all cases, however, the operator can take over and modify. A few operators prefer to work all cues manually and this would seem to be an appropriate approach for live ensemble theatre.

Top hat A short circular metal funnel in front of a spotlight (fitted in the colour runners) used, particularly in foh, to minimise any spill light and help to make the source less distinctly apparent.

Top lighting Lighting which is not necessarily so vertical as to be downlight, but which is from overhead to such an extent that little of it finds its way to the actors' eyes. Such lighting is often described as 'being a bit toppy'.

Tormentors (Torms) (1) Masking returns into the wings at the downstage limits of a set, forming what amounts to a false proscenium. (2) Spotlights mounted upstage of these tormentors, on booms (trees), or ladders.

Touring The lighting for touring productions has become increasingly sophisticated. Some small tours still travel without lights, adapting to the installations in each venue and, provided the local equipment has been well planned and is properly maintained, very good results can be obtained by a creative touring crew. However the major National companies, and other large productions with large rigs, do not wish to risk compromising their standards with technical cutbacks: every date on the tour should, as far as possible, see the same show. Moreover, artistic considerations aside, there are financial justifications for touring a lighting rig: the cost saving in time can outweigh the equipment rental and transportation charges. This is especially so if the lights are toured ready-hung on sectional trusses of manageable length for easy handling, ready-cabled for connection to a toured board with the plot on disc and requiring only minimal re-balancing in each venue.

Tracker wire The link between a liquid dimmer and its control handle was a tracker wire and these were also used for some other directly operated boards, particularly Bordonis.

Tracking The means by which a computer board charts the progress of a channel's level through a sequence of cues. As a general matter of philosophy, American boards tend to compute changing levels whereas the British record complete lighting states.

Transformation An instant scene change, often effected by exploiting the varying transparency of gauze under different lighting conditions. See BLEED.

Transformer dimmers Variable transformers were an alternative to resistance dimmers. They were load independent but expensive. See also BORDONI and VARIAC.

Translucent Material through which light, but not images, can be seen.

Transmission Transmission curves are available for each colour filter (usually printed in the swatch books) showing the percentage passed by that filter of each wavelength (ie constituent colour) in the spectrum.

Transparent Material through which images can be seen under appropriate lighting conditions.

Trees American for BOOMS.

Triac dimmers A single device which replaces the pair of thyristors normally used in a dimmer. Used only when finance dictates a cheaper alternative.

Trim American term for the height above stage level of a hanging piece of scenery, lights or masking (the equivalent in Britain is one of the meanings of DEAD.

Tripe Several cables from a lighting bar taped together until they reach the position where they are plugged into the socket outlets of the permanent wiring installation. Known as Cable Bundle in America.

Trouper A follow spot made by Strong. See also SUPER TROUPER.

Truss A framework of alloy bars and triangular cross-bracing (all of scaffolding diameter) providing a rigid structure, particularly useful for hanging lights. Used with a normal flying system when a long and/or heavily loaded spot bar would have insufficient rigidity. When suspension facilities are non-existent or inadequate, complete rigs of trussing may be hoisted and supported totally from the floor.

Tubular ripple A box with a long linear lamp and a rotating pierced cylinder to project rippling water at short range. Often used, masked by a groundrow, at the bottom of cloths.

Tungsten lamps Older type of lamps with tungsten filaments which gradually deposit particles on the glass envelope, darkening it and leading to a decline in light output.

Tungsten halogen lamps See HALOGEN. Newer lamps (now virtually standard in professional theatre) which maintain their initial brightness of light output throughout life.

Twenty-nine King Street The home of STRAND (qv) for some sixty years until the early 1970s and therefore so long the womb of British lighting technology.

Twofer See PAIRING and SPLITTER.

UV Ultra violet light (from which harmful radiations have been filtered out) used to light specially treated materials which fluoresce on an otherwise blackened stage. The standard source is a four foot UV fluorescent tube. Sometimes called 'black light'.

Up-a-point Perhaps the most frequent request from a lighting designer to a board operator.

Upstage The part of the stage furthest from the audience.

USITT (United States Institute for Theatre Technology) The American forum for theatre architects, designers and technicians to exchange information and views. There are commissions for each specialist area of technology and a major conference is held each year in a different theatrical centre across the nation.

Variable beam profile spots Profile spotlights using a zoom arrangement where the differential movement of two lens allows wide variations in both beam size and quality.

Variac The proprietary name for a brand of rotary auto-transformers used at mains voltage as dimmers, and at low voltage for mastering choke boards with a large control current requirement.

Variety A traditional variety performance, known as a variety bill, comprises a sequence of acts which follow each other without any linking material between them. Each act is a self-contained mini-production, complete with its own script, music, costumes and props. There may be one or several performers. The lighting plot is written out as a simple verbal sequence which knows only the following possibilities: full-up, blackout, red stage, blue stage, colours, pin focus, iris out and FUF (meaning full up finish). Cues are not given by a stage manager but are taken directly by the board and lime operators from information provided on their plots. These self-contained acts are often inserted into revues, summer seaside spectaculars, Christmas panto-mimes, etc, in which case the variety plots give enough information for the lighting designer to interpret lighting requirements and integrate them into the main show plot. American **Vaudeville** is similar to British Variety.

Vari*Lites Vari*Lite began life as an adjective but every-day theatre usage has rapidly changed it into a noun. These are highly sophisticated remotely controlled lighting instru-ments which use discharge lamps to provide a very intense beam. Dimming is by a motorised mechanical shutter and diffusion by motorised glass panels. Internal dichroic filters are mixed to provide a wide range of colours which, in the case of the latest models, offer a virtually unlimited choice of colours from pastels to saturates. Some models have an integral wheel for nine interchangeable gobos. Motors pro-vide movement to pan through 360° and tilt through 270° with a rotation time from 0.75 to 240 seconds. All functions are controlled by digital signals transmitted along a single circuit from a desk with memory facilities.

Vaudeville See VARIETY.

VDU (Visual Display Unit) A television type monitor screen on which all the information stored in a memory system can be displayed, including changing channel levels during a cue and channel levels as filed in any selected memory.

Virtual reality A computer aided design system where the designer, viewing a video display screen through highly sophisticated goggles, has the illusion of being inside the designed environment on the screen.

Visibility The basic first requirement of stage lighting. But see ILLUMINATION.

Voltage The world of stage lighting is divided into two by the two major alternative mains voltage supply systems of either 110/120 or 220/240. There are a number of consequences of this: perhaps the most important is that the lower voltage provides brighter lights at a given wattage but requires much heavier cable.

Ward Leonard Pioneering firm of resistance and transformer dimmer designers and manufacturers in the United States.

Warm A light in the pink-gold part of the spectrum (and therefore low in colour temperature) which tends to induce a generally comfortable atmosphere of happiness.

Wash Spotlights focused to cover wide areas, usually tinted to add colour toning in an equivalent manner to the broader brush strokes of a painter.

Water Running water may be projected with standard optical effects discs and there are reciprocating slide effects for rippling water and heaving sea. A Tubular Ripple box produces simple water ripples at the bottom of cloths from short throws. Gobos may be used with movement devices and there is a simple disc which fits small fresnels. But the simplest way to produce ripples is by reflecting light from a tray of water.

Watering can Used for the daily maintenance of liquid

dimmers by topping up the evaporation losses from prolonged running on check, particularly when heavily loaded.

Wattage The power consumption of a lamp, or the maximum available power from a dimmer. A kilowatt is 1,000 watts.

Ways The number of channels in a control system.

Wheel See DIGITAL ENCODER WHEEL.

White light The whiteness of unfiltered light, known as 'open white', varies according to the colour temperature of the lamp and the purity of the lenses. The feeling of whiteness can be assisted by the use of one of the very pale blue tints of the colour correction series of filters. Unfiltered light enjoyed a period of fashion, particularly from the late sixties to early seventies, when Brecht's theories became a cult. But Brecht's own practice was to seek the clarity of 'whiter than white' by the addition of blue tints.

Wings (1) The technical areas to the sides of the acting area. (2) Scenery standing where the acting area joins these technical areas.

Wing poles The eighteenth century equivalent of today's booms. The vertical poles upstage of the wing flats carried candles (with reflectors) whose light could be dimmed by twisting the pole away from the stage. These lighting instruments can be seen in action at DROTTNINGHOLM THEATRE (qv) where all poles are linked to a capstan in the prompt corner for coordinated movement.

Wiring The permanent wiring of a production stage lighting installation is designed to offer as much flexibility as possible by terminating in socket boxes. These are located at appropriate points for picking up the temporary cabling from instruments positioned to the requirements of the current production. As a result of voltage differences, American cable is considerably (and inconveniently) thicker than in Europe.

Woody J.T. Wood (1906–1985) whose 3-valve (one-per-phase) thyratron valve board of the early fifties, although somewhat prone to instability, opened a window on the future with its proportional cross-fading between presets and its glimpse of the multipresetting that would soon be computerised into infinite-presetting. As a pioneering exporter, Woody ensured that British stage lighting technology became familiar all over the world (saloon bar mythology has him emerging from the sea, pattern 23 in one hand and sheet of cinemoid 17 in the other).

Working lights Stage lights independent of the main production lighting system, used during rigging and rehearsals. Switched from the prompt corner, but sometimes with an overriding switch in the control room.

X, Y & Z were the letters commonly used on preset manual boards to identify the groups within each preset. On boards where groups were common to all presets, it was usual to have two groups, one identified as X, the other as Y, with a third group equivalent to, and labelled, X + Y.

Xenon Discharge lamps using xenon gas in a quartz envelope were one of the first high light output sources to supplant open carbon arcs in follow spots and scene projectors. Although still used, other discharge sources, particularly CSI, HMI and HTI have become more usual.

X-rays American term for border lights or BATTENS.

Yoke See FORK.

Zenon See XENON.

Zoom A differential movement of two lenses to alter the focal length of an optical system. In a simple zoom, the lenses are moved independently, but in more complex forms the lens are coupled so that a single movement alters the size of the beam while the image remains in constant focus. Used in advanced profile spots and scene projectors.

Pani zoom HMI followspot with louvred shutter for dimming.